Sound the Trumpet:

A Journey of Faith and Persistence

by Ron Hasselmann

with Laurie Hasselmann Ongley

ISBN: 978-1-7377329-0-7

Acknowledgments

Thank you to my daughter Laurie, who made this book a reality. Without her constant encouragement to finish writing, and then her expert editing, the project never would have been completed.

Thank you to Bill Webb for taking my scrapbooks and scanning many of the photos.

Thank you to the members of my trumpet section for being great colleagues: Charlie Schlueter, Manny Laureano, Clem Volpe, and Mike Hipps.

Thank you to members of my tour posse who are no longer around to reminisce about the old days: Steve Zellmer, Frank Winsor, and Bernie Adelstein.

Thank you to my teachers Ren Schilke, who shared his house with me, encouraged me to practice, and sent overflow gigs my way; Bud Herseth, who showed me how to be an orchestral player; and Arnold Jacobs, who probed my technical problems and made me a better teacher. Thank you to my many students, from whom I learned more than I taught.

Thank you to the Minnesota Orchestra for being so much more than an employer. Thank you to the Lake Wobegon® Brass Band for providing a musical family at the end of my professional playing days.

Thank you to Wes Gebhardt, my buddy for over 80 years.

This book is dedicated to my sister Jean, who passed away as the project was nearing completion.

Contents

Not Famous, But—

In the 118 years from 1903, when the Minneapolis Symphony was founded, to 2021 and the modern Minnesota Orchestra, there have been only ten music directors at the helm:

Emil Oberhoffer	1903–1922
Henri Verbrugghen	1923–1931
Eugene Ormandy	1931–1936
Dimitri Mitropoulos	1937–1949
Antal Dorati	1949–1960
Stanislaw Skrowaczewski	1960–1979
Neville Marriner	1979–1986
Edo de Waart	1986–1995
Eiji Oue	1996–2002
Osmo Vänskä	2003–

To the best of my knowledge, I am the only person who has played for all of the orchestra's music directors except Oberhoffer and Verbrugghen, both of whom were deceased by the time I was born. My career with the orchestra began in the fall of 1958 when I was hired by music director Antal Dorati. I was Associate Principal Trumpet until I retired in 2000, playing regular concerts for Dorati, Skrowaczewski, Marriner, de Waart, and Oue. My first performances with Mitropoulos occurred during the 1956 season of the Lyric Opera in Chicago, where I played first trumpet for two years. Ormandy guest-conducted in Minnesota several times during my tenure. After retirement I was called to fill in under Vänskä, once as an extra and once as a substitute.

Playing for eight of the ten conductors of the Minneapolis Symphony/ Minnesota Orchestra has made me uniquely positioned to reminisce about the orchestra. I have met thousands of musicians in Minnesota, both staff and visitors. I hope their memories of the orchestra are as fond as mine are.

Bob Dorer speaking in honor of my retirement from the Minnesota Orchestra, Orchestra Hall lobby, 1999

Grade-school portrait with my sister Jean

My Main Street: Lowell Avenue, Chicago

The bell toll for my entry into this world was on March 3, 1933. I was born in a bungalow on Lowell Avenue in Chicago, and lived in the same house until I was drafted into the Army. Lowell Avenue was a two-block-long street separated by railroad tracks from the Schwinn bicycle factory. The other end of the street was Armitage Avenue, a busy thoroughfare where ancient red and yellow streetcars lumbered along every five minutes.

All of the houses on our block were identical, built of Chicago brick, with eight steps embraced on either side by two concrete slabs. In the days before air conditioning, these slabs were comfortable resting places where neighbors could gather nightly for fellowship and gossip. The houses were spaced eight feet apart with a cement walkway, called a "gangway," between. Every now and then when heavy rains flooded our street, we would sit on the front steps and watch boaters row up and down from one end of the street to the other. On summer nights, we could hear exuberant shouting from the church on the corner of Lowell and Cortland. We didn't know the denomination of the congregation, but all the kids in the neighborhood referred to them as the "Holy Rollers," probably parroting our parents.

On Halloween night, older kids unknown to us would haul a huge wooden box onto the streetcar tracks on Armitage Avenue and set fire to it when the streetcar was a block away. One year when the motorman got out of the streetcar to pull the box off the tracks, another kid who was on the streetcar closed the door and drove off with the motorman chasing and the passengers screaming hysterically. We little kids witnessed this event from our humdrum ritual of soaping store windows.

Our street was especially beautiful in the spring and summer months

With my sister, father, grandparents Mary and Henry Hasselmann (L), and Aunt Ida and Uncle Fred (R)

because everyone tried to outdo their neighbors with beautiful landscaping and lawns. Not to be outdone, my dad brought home a truckload of manure from my Uncle George's mushroom farm and spread it over our lawn. The natural fertilizer was not a problem until it rained, and the humidity rose. Then the air was so full of the smell of animal dung, and the air so blue, that passing neighbors crossed the street to keep from gagging on the odor. We did, however, have the most beautiful lawn for many blocks around.

My uncles and their farms were integral parts of my childhood. I remember Uncle Al pumping a cow's tail, insisting that this was how he got milk out of her. At Uncle Ed's farm I couldn't resist climbing high up outside the silo. I thought it would be cool to jump from the top into the corn piled high below. I was lucky that Uncle Ed saw me, and as I jumped he caught my clothing halfway down and held me fast. Ed explained that if I had gone into the corn, there was a good chance that I would have smothered to death.

Back in Chicago, one snowy winter evening my dad hitched our red wagon to the back bumper of his car and pulled my sister and me down Lowell Avenue, much to our squealing delight.

The backyard of my house was my world in these early years: a grassy area 30 yards by 30 yards, surrounded by a garage, a back porch, and two neighborhood fences. These were happy days for me as I looked out from the yard and viewed life in all its glory. The alley behind our house provided endless adventures. Frequently a horse-drawn wagon would stop by our house and deliver blocks of ice for our icebox. Weekly, another horse-drawn wagon would travel down the alley with the driver shouting, "Rags, old iron, rags, old iron." This was a time to unload any items no longer being used and a chance to haggle.

I especially enjoyed watching Dad negotiating the best deal for his unused goods and my grandmother scooping up the horse droppings after the peddlers had left to spread on her flower garden. Grandma always had the most beautiful garden in the neighborhood.

Another weekly event was the visit from the sanitation workers who shoveled out the garbage from our square cement box. In those days Chicago homes didn't have freestanding trash cans, but built-in cement containers with lift-up lids in back of people's yards, facing the alleys. Naturally this provided a haven for rats, which regularly infiltrated the containers. Rodents would also make their home in our garage, which was a storehouse for all of Dad's treasures. All the time I lived in Chicago, no car

With my sister Jean as young children

ever saw the inside of our two-car garage. It was packed full of stuff, including a collection of 55-gallon drums filled with wax that belonged to my Uncle Elmer, who was in the wax business. I never did understand why we stored these drums, even keeping empty barrels in our basement. When heavy rain came and flooded our basement, the empty drums would float around and bang together like some chain gang trying to shake off their shackles. Once in a while Dad would clean out the garage and set Jean and me up on the drums while he worked. Happy, our black fox terrier and ever-vigilant ratter, sniffed each section of the garage as Dad pulled away items from the walls, finally reaching the last corner where Happy was sure her prey was hiding. She was never disappointed: the moment the last object was removed, a rat would inevitably race out around the drums where Jean and I were ensconced, with Happy chasing the rat not far behind. It was never long before Happy had her victim clenched tightly in her teeth, and ended the drama with a triumphant snap of her head.

From my backyard I could watch the trains with their billowing black smoke chug by a half block away. Mondays were always wash days, and my grandmother would hang the clothes out to dry. If the wind was coming from the south, occasionally the soot from the train smoke would land on the wet clothes and she had to repeat the washing process all over again.

In the summer, my sister Jean and I spent hot afternoons running through the sprinkler. No swimming pool for us. We didn't know we were poor—we were happy with each other and our own way of beating the heat. I also enjoyed rolling around on the newly cut grass. Sometimes my dad would mow the lawn just before a big storm. I would roll around looking up at the big dark clouds gathering, and see how long I could stay outside before the first drops of rain hit my head.

One year, as I was playing in the backyard on a bright sunny day, the sky suddenly became overcast. As I looked up to see why, I saw that the sun was blocked out by a huge cigar-shaped object. It was a dirigible floating quietly and peacefully overhead. I often wondered, years later, if that had been the Hindenburg, Germany's pride in the late 1930s.

World War II was a tangible presence in my childhood. My family dutifully practiced nighttime blackouts and air raid drills, and we contributed to paper and scrap drives. My friends and I ran all over the neighborhood to capture simulated bombs dropped by parachutes. My mother adjusted her daily menus to accommodate food rationing. Because my father, an embalmer, had to travel for work, he received a priority B sticker, which entitled him to more gas than the standard ration.

It was safe in those carefree days to walk down our street at all hours of the day or early evening. Even as small children, we could walk up to the store on Armitage Avenue by ourselves to purchase a gallon of milk, or to the candy store for some penny candy. One of my favorite stores was the butcher shop, where I could make drawings in the sawdust on the floor.

My "gang" of closest friends from school and church all lived on my block: Eddy, Wes, Edie, and Roy. We roller-skated together and played "three feet off," baseball with sewer covers as bases, football, cops and robbers, and cowboys and Indians, and we acted out every childhood fantasy we could think of.

One of my neighbors and I each had a white rabbit, and we were under the impression that they were both male. When Tony moved, he gave me his rabbit. One day when I went to clean out the hutch, I discovered eight little pink baby bunnies, all dead. You can imagine what that did to my biological mind, thinking two male rabbits could produce babies. My father, a professional embalmer, was the logical person to talk to about death and proper burial procedures. From him I procured several bottles of embalming fluid. I swirled the bunnies around in a bucket, placed each of them in little matchboxes, and set them gently into my little red wagon.

My parents Evelyn and Emil Hasselmann as a young couple

I called my neighborhood friends to attend a simple service, followed by a parade down the center of Lowell Avenue. Leading the parade was Eddy carrying a hastily created American flag drawn with crayons and tied to a long stick. Wes and I followed, shouldering Red Ryder BB guns, and my sister pulled the wagon as a stand-in for a hearse. We arrived back at my house for the burial in the backyard, where eight little graves had been prepared. We had a short scripture and prayer, then the firing of the BB guns followed by my playing "Taps" on the bugle. My sentimental sister played the part (quite realistically) of the mourner. I moved the two adult rabbits to separate cages, but to my surprise, soon more baby rabbits appeared. Once again, my biological mind went into a tailspin. These babies survived, so I had to build more and more cages, until I eventually had thirty-five rabbits. To feed this horde, I swept out boxcars from a neighboring grain elevator, and I picked up crates of carrot tops from a local grocery store. On Saturdays, my friends and I would let all the rabbits run loose in my fenced yard, both for their exercise and to let them trim the grass.

It wasn't until many years later that I discovered the answer to the mystery of the rabbit babies. My dad eventually confessed that he and his friends had amused themselves by giving the rabbits visiting privileges after I had gone to bed. This proliferation of rabbits occurred during the Second World War, when meat was in short supply, so I finally quit my rabbit-tending efforts and furnished my neighborhood with hasenpfeffer.

Clerking at the record store during a visit from Evelyn Knight

At the age of 11, I began my working career with the *Downtown Shopping News,* a free newspaper to be rubber-banded securely to the doorknob of each house every Wednesday and Saturday. This meant walking up every staircase of all 411 houses on my route. Halfway through the route I always came home to eat half a loaf of my grandmother's fresh-baked bread, which had steamed up all the windows. I vividly remember walking eight blocks to pick up my papers for the first time. After loading them carefully into my red wagon I immediately dumped them all over the street as I tried to negotiate a high curb. All this for 90 cents a route! The money I earned weekly for my effort was divided thus: 10¢ for a new balsa wood model airplane, 15¢ for soda and candy, and the balance to purchase war savings bonds stamps. When I had saved $18.75 I bought a war bond redeemable for $25.00 in 10 years. Later I was promoted to Captain, which meant that the papers for my four routes were delivered to my house for an additional 40 cents per day. Much later I was promoted to Inspector, which meant that I was to ride around on my bike to make sure the paperboys were making their deliveries in the appropriate manner. I was also required to interview customers in three houses to ensure they were happy with their service, and write up a report each week. The Inspector's pay was $1.50 twice a week. After five years of this commitment, I was offered a job at Shapiro's drug store on Irving Park Road, near Kelvyn Park High School.

Following my job at Shapiro's I worked at a local record store owned by Andy Anderson, where I probably spent more money on jazz and classical records than I made in salary. When the Schwann Catalog was still in its infancy, I had the distinction of owning every record in the catalog! I can still recall that the first 78 record I bought was trumpeter Rafael Méndez playing *Flight of the Bumblebee,* and my first LP was the soundtrack to *South Pacific.* From time to time, recording artists visited our shop to sign autographs and delight wall-to-wall adoring fans. In the 1950s I recall visits from Vic Damone, Frankie Laine, and Evelyn Knight.

Throughout my childhood I calculated money in nickels. The Good Humor truck offered ice cream treats for a nickel, so that became my unit of measurement.

Sunday mornings were reserved for church at St. Timothy Lutheran, where the opening hymn was always "Holy, Holy, Holy." The men and boys sat on the left side of the church, the women and girls on the right. I played solo hymns during the evening fireside hour, and my sister Jean played piano. My mom wrote out more hymns while we played. She knew to transpose the notes up a step, because I was playing a B-flat horn, but she didn't know to add two sharps. I played a lot of wrong notes.

At Sunday school after the service, the closeness of our neighborhood gang solidified. Wes, Eddy, Edie, Else, Jimmy, and several other kids from our street all belonged to the same church. Wes and I had a special friendship, and did very few things without including the other. Our friendship remains solid to this day, even though we live over 400 miles apart.

Many Sunday afternoons Wes and I would go to the movies, either the Tiffin Theater on North Avenue, the Karlov Theater on Armitage Avenue, or the Liberty Theater on Fullerton Avenue. The Karlov was only a few blocks from our houses, but we most often chose the Liberty because they usually showed three features (mostly cowboy movies), several cartoons, an ongoing short serial, and news of the world, all for 11 cents! Our difficult decision at the end of the show was whether to leave then and get the free comic book offered by the theater, or stay to see the whole show over again. We took both options many times.

I remember the day I received a BB gun as a gift. I sat on the back steps of our house with Wes and a few other friends shooting at the silver wind turbine on the roof of the garage. After we all took several turns, I saw a robin sitting on the fence across the alley from our yard. To me it was nothing more than another target. I took careful aim, fired, and hit the bird. It gave a little croak and fell into the alley. We ran up to it, and everyone shouted, "YOU KILLED IT!" I was horrified. I had never killed anything, nor had I intended to this time. We buried the poor thing; I went into the house, put the BB gun away, and never shot it again, except at the rabbit funeral.

It was hard to come back to Lowell Avenue last year after an absence of forty years. All my friends have moved away except Eddy, who recently died. My former home now has several broken and boarded-up windows. The two front trees that we loved to climb are no longer there. The grass that I trimmed with the care of a manicurist is now all dirt and trash. The garage that I painted many times, once surrounded by rabbit hutches, had burned down. The PT boat that I carved into the asphalt in front of the house is still visible, although worn down. I don't know that I would feel as safe walking down Lowell Avenue today as I did in my youth.

The memories of my friends and family will be with me forever, but I have no desire to return again to my "Main Street."

Making krumkake with my mother Evelyn

Lane Technical High School Brass Sextet: (L to R) R. Hasselmann, W. Andronowitz, R. Martin, R. Wyzykowski, R. Clavijo, J. Rothermel

A Musical Awakening

My first awareness that music could touch my soul came from the tri-weekly radio show *The Lone Ranger*. I was thrilled by the heroic trumpet call (taken from Gioachino Rossini's *William Tell Overture,* I later learned) as the hero rode off into the distance with a hearty, "Hi-Yo, Silver! Away!" I couldn't wait for each Monday, Wednesday, and Friday at 6:30 p.m., to be regaled with another adventure of our hero bringing law and order to the frontier. Of course I had to drink the sponsored commercial product, Ovaltine, and send for the special decoder ring to decipher the secret messages that only dedicated members could decode from the Lone Ranger.

In the early 1940s I advanced to a new musical adventure, tuning in to a weekly half-hour radio show of classical selections on Sundays at 7 p.m. I must have been devoted to this show, because I recall several occasions when I made a fuss with my parents when we were visiting my grandparents and I missed the broadcast. My dad sensed my budding interest in music and bought a plastic bugle for me. It wasn't long before my parents realized the limitations of the plastic instrument, and they started shopping for a cornet. They consulted

Consumer Reports, which listed a Besson model made in France as top choice. A clerk at the music store said (inaccurately) that there was no such name, and that my parents must have meant "Blessing," a trumpet made in Texas. They paid $105 and presented this horn to me at Christmas.

I attended William Penn Nixon Grade school on the north side of Chicago. No band or any instrumental instruction was available, so playing in church was my only regular performance opportunity. Somehow I was invited to play with the Norwood Park Symphony Orchestra, the youngest member by far.

I attended Kelvyn Park High School only for my freshman year. There I played in the orchestra under the direction of Mrs. Fischer. This was a frustrating experience, because my musical experience had outpaced the freshman-year repertoire and the abilities of my classmates. After a year of attending the high school in my district, I was eligible to transfer to Lane Technical High School, at that time an all boys' school with a fantastic reputation for music. Lane boasted five music teachers, a fine orchestra, two bands, and courses in harmony, theory, counterpoint, orchestration, and music history. I was accepted into the concert band, although I began as number 10 in the line of cornet players. My band director, G. P. Huff, was a former saxophone player with Wayne King's Orchestra. I also played in the Lane Orchestra, directed by Paul Schneider, and the ROTC marching band, directed by Mr. Grill. By the end of my third year at Lane I had worked my way up to solo cornet in the concert band. One of my most vivid memories is from a band contest, when a tight-fisted cymbal player swung and missed. The impact sent him into a spiral move, and he crashed down on the timpani player on a lower riser. This was the only occasion during my time at Lane that we received an E (excellent) rating instead of our usual S (superior).

Early Playing Gigs

In Chicago during World War II, members of my family, like all patriotic citizens, practiced the required wartime drills. We pulled down our window shades at night to keep enemy planes from spotting our lights and bombing the city. It was customary for people who had sons, brothers, or fathers serving in the military to display in their front window a white 8" × 10" flag with a red border and a blue star in the center. When the terrible news of a loved one's death touched the doorsteps of a home, the blue star was replaced with a gold star, and the local VFW arranged a memorial service to be held in front of the home. Typically, these services included a chaplain, an honor guard, and occasionally a drum and bugle corps.

As a bugler in the Northwest Drum and Bugle Corps, I sometimes participated in these services. I played my first memorial while still a junior high school student. The Corps paraded all around the neighborhood while playing, both to honor the fallen soldier and to draw people out from their homes to be part of the service. My job that day, in addition to parading, was to play an echo of "Taps," which was played right after the rifle salute. (The newest member of the group always got the job of playing the echo.) Before the service started, I asked the bugler playing the main "Taps" part, a high school senior, what I was supposed to do as the echo. He looked down the street and pointed, saying, "You go down the street about four houses, and when I play a phrase, you play the same thing right after me, so it sounds like an echo." I thought, "I can do that," so I walked down the sidewalk, past four houses, and took up my position, waiting for the rifle shots and the other bugler's first phrase.

Ready to march, with my cousin Marilyn Highgate (L) and my sister Jean

At last, the rifles fired. The high school kid played the first three notes of "Taps" from his location, but badly clammed the third note. Because my job was to echo what he did, I played the same three notes, and I muffed the third one, just as he had done. He played the second phrase, and once again, he clammed the third note. Just trying to do my job, I echoed again, including the slippery third note. The big kid struggled through the rest of the song, and to me he sounded increasingly strained. I could tell that he was becoming more and more frustrated. I continued to echo everything I heard.

When it was over, I walked back to the rest of the group. The older bugler grabbed my arm and shook me, saying, "Why were you making fun of me?" I

Dressed for my graduation from grade school

carefully explained that I was just doing what I was told, echoing what I had heard; otherwise, it wouldn't be a true echo. The bigger guy would have pounded me into the sidewalk if it hadn't been for other members of the group, who stepped in and defused the situation.

I wasn't always the pre-professional that I liked to consider myself. The Northwest Drum and Bugle Corps was scheduled to march several miles in a big parade down Michigan Avenue, a major street in downtown Chicago. It so happened that the only cornet mouthpiece I owned was used by both my single-valved bugle and my cornet. In my haste to hurry downtown I forgot to transfer the mouthpiece from my cornet case to my bugle bag. Consequently, I marched the entire parade holding my bugle up without playing a note.

My sight-reading skill as a teenager owed much to an Italian feast band I played in when I was 13. On summer feast days, a parade through the Italian section of Chicago was accompanied by a band playing marches, wearing white shirts and military-style caps. We assembled before a Catholic church around 9 a.m. and began parading, or rather strolling, down the street. The music was played at about 132 on the metronome, but we strolled at around 72. In front of the band, four men carried a statue of the Virgin Mary with streamers of ribbons cascading down from her shoulders. As we paraded, neighbors ran up and pinned or clipped money onto those streamers. Occasionally someone would call out to the marchers something in Italian, and the band would gather in front of that house and play a special tune. We were rewarded with a red-hued alcoholic beverage poured from a jug into little tin cups that most of the musicians had tucked in their pockets. Since I was the only kid in the band, sometimes a bottle of Orange Crush was offered to me. The parade passed by many food booths offering an abundance of Italian dishes as well as clothing and trinkets. We broke for an hour for lunch, then resumed parading. After a dinner break, around 7 p.m. we would play a concert on a temporary band shell. The repertoire was mostly opera overtures such as Hérold's *Zampa* and Rossini's *Italian in Algiers*. Music for the concert was standard sheet music, but the parade marches were all hand-written manuscripts copied and bound in 1939.

I don't remember how I got tapped for this job, but I do recall that at the end of each event, I was told the time and location of the next one. I had no contact information—I simply reported at the appointed street corner at the appointed date and time and we would set off. I was paid $8 or $9 for the day, which seemed to me like a generous wage. One morning I took a streetcar to the intersection where I had been told to report, and nobody was there. I found no parade, no band. I had no phone number to call, so I went home and waited for a call about the next parade. The call never came, so I unceremoniously ended my career in Italian parades. I did have a consolation prize, though: I had no way to return my book of beautiful handwritten music, which I still own.

By the time I was in high school, I played in a combo led by my long-time friend Dick Wildberger, who played accordion, along with a sax player and a drummer. We were hired for many weddings and dances, but one dance in particular remains embedded in my memory. It was a warm evening in a large room over a tavern in North Chicago. There was no air conditioning at that time and the room was overcrowded, hot, and smoky. We had just finished playing a long set and were taking a break. I took my chance to get some fresh air by sitting on the window sill overlooking the street. I noticed a big convertible Cadillac pull up in front of the tavern below us. I called to my colleagues, "Look at those guys below," pointing out the four big shoulder-to-shoulder men in black suits with large black hats. We could hear their heavy footsteps coming up the stairs. The biggest guy, smoking a fat cigar, came up to us and demanded, "You guys union?" We replied, "No, but we are saving our money to join." He said, "Good boys, you be in the union next time we come around, or there won't be a next time." The following Monday morning we went downtown and joined the musicians' union. These were the days when James Petrillo ruled the Chicago musicians' union with an iron hand. It was well known that Petrillo sent goon squads around the city looking for working bands not belonging to the union. Band members who were warned and chose not to be intimidated were frequently beaten up and had their instruments smashed. One friend of ours who played in another band showed us his drum set after he was visited by the mob: mangled drum heads and shattered pieces of wood all over the street. One of the trumpet players' horns had been smashed around a telephone pole into a U shape. The police were unresponsive.

Whitehorse, Wisconsin, in 1952 with the founding members of the Chicago Symphony Brass Quintet: (L to R) Renold Schilke, Arnold Jacobs, Adolph Herseth, Frank Crisafulli, Hugh Cowden

Chicago Symphony

I was a member of the Minneapolis Symphony/Minnesota Orchestra for forty-two years, but my love of music originated with my first "home" orchestra, the Chicago Symphony Orchestra. I first heard the CSO when I was in the fourth grade and I attended a Young People's Concert. I remember sitting in one of the box balcony seats without a clue what I was about to experience. Our teachers hadn't told us whether we were going to hear a lecture, watch a ballet, or see something entirely different. The first clue came when I looked down and saw some percussion instruments on stage. Then, one by one, people with instruments came on stage and began to warm up with scales and arpeggios.

When all the musicians were present, the conductor came out and gave a downbeat for a drumroll. The orchestra began to play the "Star-Spangled Banner"—what a glorious sound that was! My soul leapt upward and my life-long love affair with orchestral music began.

My next memorable contact with the Chicago Symphony took place when I was a senior in high school. For the finale of another Young People's Concert, the orchestra invited Chicago's top high school players to participate in the finale, Tchaikovsky's *1812 Overture*. I still have the letter from the Board of Education's director of music to my high school principal, requesting permission for me to miss school to attend a rehearsal and concert with the orchestra. How proud I was, sitting in the choir seats behind the brass section! I remember watching first trumpet Adolph Herseth as he warmed up and played. To this day, I can picture him sitting in front of me in his rehearsal shirt, a red-and-black checked flannel. I was also amused to learn that during long periods of rehearsal when he didn't play, Herseth read *Field and Stream* magazine. We high school kids played our hearts out, of course. We finished the performance to thunderous applause, and Herseth turned around and gave us a thumbs-up. I had never been so happy.

Several years later, I sang the Verdi Requiem with the Northwestern University Glee Club and the CSO, Bruno Walter conducting. Again, I performed from the choir risers behind the brass section. I was deeply moved by the Verdi concert, which inspired in me a new appreciation for operatic singing. A few years after this performance, when I read Walter's obituary, I discovered that he had been a protégé of Gustav Mahler, the great Austrian composer whose music I have grown to love passionately. Little did I realize when I shook Maestro Walter's hand that I had shaken a hand that had touched the hand of Gustav Mahler. It was another great moment in my life, even though I appreciated it only after the fact.

Still at Northwestern, I was hired as one of four off-stage trumpeters for another performance of the Verdi Requiem. We extra players were from four different colleges, unknown to each other. The conductor, Fritz Reiner, had a reputation as a tyrant who would not tolerate the slightest mistake. Our part answered Herseth's solo entrances. At the first rehearsal he played and we answered, but we were out of tune. He played again, and we responded, again out of tune. Reiner stopped the rehearsal and said to Herseth, "Take those trumpet players off in a room and work to get them in tune." He paused and looked down at his music stand. Then he added, "If you don't get them in tune in a half hour, find four other trumpet players." We grew up fast that day! This was my introduction to the Big Time, where a rehearsal prepared for a concert *tonight*. I was accustomed to high school and college, where months might be spent preparing a program. We worked it out, and Reiner left us alone for the rest of the week. He was famous for not complimenting anyone, so we felt that we had done our job. This time, I felt relief to get a thumbs-up from Herseth.

An aside about Fritz Reiner: The entire orchestra knew of his reputation for not offering up compliments. One day after the entire orchestra executed a particularly difficult passage, he muttered, "Good." The orchestra, in a frenzy of excitement, clapped and shouted happily. After calm was restored, Reiner said, "But not that good."

One summer I was living with Ren Schilke (then a player in the CSO, now known as the founder of the Schilke trumpet company) while I painted his house in Evanston. The money I earned by painting was earmarked for my fall tuition at Northwestern. CSO brass players Herseth, Arnold Jacobs (tuba), Frank Crisafulli (trombone), and Hugh Cowden (horn) came to Ren's house to form the inaugural Chicago Symphony Brass Quintet, specifically to prepare for a week-long tour throughout Wisconsin. As the quintet rehearsed in the living room, I kept leaning over to

Ren Schilke (L) and Bud Herseth

hear them through an open window. Jacobs was convinced I was going to fall onto the concrete driveway, so he told Ren, "Get that kid off the ladder before he breaks his neck." Ren asked me to come in, still in my painting clothes, and sit in a corner and listen. After another hour of rehearsing they had worked up a solid program, with the exception of a grand finale. Ren pulled out the Bohme Sextet, and when Hugh asked how they could play it with only five players, Ren told me to get my trumpet. In the end, I was invited along on the Wisconsin tour as the sixth man in the quintet and a part-time stagehand. My fondest recollection of the week was traveling by train with Jacobs to northern Wisconsin, after the others had driven up earlier. We spent the entire ride in the club car, where Jake discussed brass technique and held me completely captivated. His concepts and scholarly descriptions were so far above me that I was afraid to ask any questions and break the spell.

Back at home I managed to take only four lessons from Jake before I was drafted into the Army, but after I returned I studied with him for several years. He completely broke down my breathing technique, with explanations of the cerebral cortex, the diaphragm, the 8th and 9th and 10th ribs, and intercostal muscles. After I became a professional player I continued to take occasional lessons from Jake whenever I could.

Many years later, the Minnesota Orchestra and the Chicago Symphony were in New York at the same time. We were all preparing for concerts at Carnegie Hall, and as tradition and hunger would have it, some of the brass players from both orchestras ran into each other at Carnegie Deli. Crisafulli greeted me with, "There's the 6th man!" (I'm not sure Crisafulli ever remembered my name, but he did remember that I was the "6th man.") Jacobs started talking about technique, and a whole gaggle of brass players hung on every word until 3 a.m. The Doctor of Brass Playing held a regular seminar on breathing right there in the Carnegie Deli, where his deep voice and long wisdom held us all spellbound.

Cross-country skiing, 1970s

Who Needs a Music Major, Anyway?

As my senior year in high school was drawing to a close, my band director asked me what I was going to study in college. "Music," I said without hesitation. He objected, "Why? You can't make a living in music." I reported this conversation to my father, who agreed with the teacher and suggested that I apply to Northwestern University Business School. Dad was an embalmer, and if I got a business degree, he and I could open a funeral parlor together. That plan sounded sensible: "You never saw a poor funeral director," and I could keep playing gigs on the side.

I enrolled in Business Administration at Northwestern and studied enthusiastically. Joining the Delta Sigma Pi fraternity, I was surrounded by a group of business students who encouraged and helped me, but to no avail. No matter how hard I studied and avoided parties, my grades the first quarter set me up to fail. With grades of two Cs and two Ds, I was placed on probation. Padding my transcript with typing and other easy courses, I got removed from probation and returned to the business courses. Repeat results, only this time it was three Ds and a C. I came home and lamented to my father, "Dad, I'm going to flunk out of college if I continue on this path." With words still ringing in my ears he said, "I understand, just go follow your dream!" I didn't know exactly what my dream was. I just knew that I wanted to play my horn. The third quarter, after changing my major to Music Education, my grades rose to As and Bs.

My reasoning for an education major rather than performance was simple. If I applied for a performance job, the audition committee would care only about how well I played. If I applied for a college or high

My high school graduation portrait

school teaching position, a college degree would be required. I couldn't practice any more than I was already doing while taking education courses, so I had nothing to lose.

At Northwestern from 1950 to 1954, I played in the marching band, the concert band, and the symphony orchestra. For three years I also played in the Broadway-style Waa-Mu shows in the spring. Off campus, I joined a 1930s-style 13-piece dance band led by Jimmy Featherstone. We played for open dance hall dancing on weekends, mostly out of town. We often left Chicago in the early afternoon and traveled to locations such as Vermilion, Ohio; Terre Haute, Indiana; and Arnolds Park in Lake Okoboji, Iowa. We also played frequently at the Naval Station Great Lakes, north of Chicago, on Friday nights for enlisted men and on Saturday nights for officers. Each out-of-town gig paid $25. I figured that when I counted the hours we spent driving to and from the job, we averaged $1 an hour. I didn't care—I was playing my horn, having fun, and making money.

The summers of 1953 and 1954 were spent on the road with Barnes and Caruthers grandstand shows at state fairs throughout the Midwest, one week at a time. These were variety shows with dancers in lavish costumes, magicians, comics, and jugglers. Our orchestra or dance band played throughout the evening shows and also played for the afternoon races of cars and trotters. We would play for half an hour before the race and then sit around playing cards until a siren announced a wreck. We would race upstairs to the stage and play music while the wreck was being cleared from the track.

During my junior year in college the Korean War was still raging. I knew that when I completed my education I would be drafted, so I planned a trip to Washington to audition for some of the service bands. I contacted the Army Band, but they would be on tour the week of my visit. The Navy Band did not have any openings at that time. I managed to arrange auditions for the Marine Band and the Air Force Band on the same day in May, 1953.

My audition for the Marine Band was held in the band room with only the band director, the famous Lt. Colonel Santelmann, listening. He asked me to play something I knew, so I began with Hindemith's sonata for trumpet to show my playing power. Then I played a lyrical section from Jean Hubeau's sonata and finally a part of the Giannini trumpet concerto, all works I was preparing for recitals at Northwestern. After a while he looked at me strangely and said, "Don't you know anything I would recognize?" Then it hit me: he was brought up on Sousa and band music. What had I been thinking? I played Arban's *Carnival of Venice* with a few variations, and he said, "Now I know you're a good cornet player. Why didn't you play that before instead of all that other crap?" It was at that point that I learned, "Always know who your audience will be."

Santelmann then asked me what string instrument I was proficient on. I told him I only knew the basics of string playing from my music education courses. He told me he had plenty of cornet players but he needed someone who could double on strings for small chamber ensembles. So I didn't pass the audition. I found out later that he had been a solo violinist, and there was an old dual band/orchestra rule that called for string players to double on a brass instrument and vice versa.

One down, one to go. In the afternoon I met with Colonel Mitchell, director of the United States Air Force Band. After a brief interview, he placed some music before me and complimented me on my performance. He indicated that he could use me in the band, but as my excitement rose, he dashed my hopes with his reluctance to issue a letter to me acknowledging my acceptance into the band. He said instead that when I returned home to Chicago, I should go down to the Air Force recruiting office and enlist, telling them all that had happened in Washington. I don't know why he thought I was naive enough to sign away four years of my life, probably ending up in a post band in North Dakota or on some battleship, but I declined the offer.

In 1954 my draft number came up, and I left the grandstand tour to begin my new career and adventure as Army private.

Brass players in the 7th Army Symphony: (L to R) Gene Lewis, Dick Judson, me, Cloud Crawford

The Luck of a Soldier

My mother taught me early on how to handle a disappointment: "When one door closes, a better one will always open." This maxim proved to be true when I entered the United States Army in 1954. In my fourth week of basic training at Camp Chaffee, Arkansas, I had the opportunity to audition for the post band. I failed the audition with a sergeant, which disappointed and surprised me, as I had played principal trumpet in my university orchestra. I expected that this band must be fabulous, if I wasn't good enough to play in it. However, I heard their concert a week later and discovered that the sergeant who auditioned me was the principal trumpeter in the band, and a poor one at that. He was obviously afraid to lose his solo position if I joined the band.

Not yet dismayed, in my twelfth week of basic training I wrote a letter to the Fourth Army headquarters requesting an assignment to their band. The Fourth Army band director sent my request letter back to my company commander, who summoned me to his office. He asked me if I remembered the "chain of command" that I had been introduced to several weeks earlier: a soldier starts all requests with his sergeant, who sends it to the captain, then to the post commander, who will, if he deems it appropriate, forward it to the other company. I had violated this procedure by going over all their heads. The commander asked for my liberty pass, and instructed me to tear it into as many pieces as I could. For the next four weeks, while my colleagues went into Fort Smith, Arkansas, for weekends, I guarded prisoners and worked in the grease pits, scraping the underside of Army trucks.

Graduation from basic training finally came, and we stood outside our barracks waiting for future assignments. Some were assigned to Korea, some to the Marshall Islands, Panama, the United States, Alaska (not yet a state), and Europe. I held my breath, until I heard my name and the word "Europe." I was elated! However, my excitement was short-lived because in clearing the post, I didn't have my two pairs of Army-issued glasses. My class went off without me, while I had to wait two weeks for my new glasses and the next graduation class. I was back guarding prisoners and scraping the underside of trucks. Once again I held my breath and was relieved to hear "Europe" called out after my name.

Because I was a college graduate, the Army assumed that I could type. I was assigned to the 385th Military Police Battalion in Böblingen, Germany, as a clerk typist. Each morning at 6:30 a.m., my fellow soldiers and I would march around the courtyard in close-order drill. Most of the soldiers were not draftees as I was, and spent their time training to be tough policemen. I did not share their machismo, so at my first opportunity I borrowed a Jeep and looked up a fellow trumpet player in the Seventh Army Symphony. He arranged an audition for me, and I was accepted.

Armed with a letter requesting my immediate transfer to the orchestra, I presented myself to my commanding officer. He asked what instrument I played, and when I said trumpet, he informed me that he had been searching for someone with my qualifications to help him form a drum and bugle corps. There were sixteen bugles and ten drums in the basement; the colonel asked me if I would watch morning drill and identify the twenty-six best marchers, and then, after he requisitioned them for the corps, teach them to play their instruments. I panicked inwardly, but thanked him for the offer. He told me to report back the next morning at 0600 hours with my decision. I borrowed the Jeep again and headed for Seventh Army headquarters. The symphony conductor, a corporal, heard my dilemma and took me to the office of the commanding general of the Seventh Army, General Anthony McAuliffe. (This was the commander who replied "Nuts!" to the Germans' surrender ultimatum at the Battle of the Bulge.) The conductor told the general, "I need this man for my orchestra, and a bird colonel down the road won't let me have him."

The Seventh Army Symphony was a pet project of General McAuliffe's, having been formed two years before at the suggestion of Dimitri Mitropoulos, then the conductor of the New York Philharmonic. Mitropoulos had heard the comment, "Americans have no culture—just listen to their hillbilly music on the radio," and had the idea of an Army symphony to change Europeans' minds about us. There was also a dearth of live orchestral music in Europe, with most professional musicians having been killed, maimed, or captured in the war.

7th Army Symphony rehearsing in Paris in 1955, Ronald Ondrejka conducting

When he heard about my dilemma, General McAuliffe told the conductor, "No problem!" and issued a memo saying, "This man *will* be transferred, by order of General McAuliffe." With glee, I took my letter of transfer back to base and apologized to the colonel for not accepting the opportunity he offered me.

The next eighteen months were like a European vacation. One week of rehearsals, then three weeks of touring around Europe playing concerts. No guard duty, no KP, no duties at all except to play music. We performed all over

Germany, France, Holland, Belgium, Luxembourg, and Denmark. We played to ecstatic audiences. When we had relief or vacation time, we traveled to Switzerland, Italy, and England.

I have often wondered what would have happened if any of the other "opportunities" had panned out. I caught a glimpse of one possibility: if I had not lost my glasses and had shipped out with my first basic training class, I would have been assigned to France. There was no reciprocal transferring between the German command and the French, and at best I would have played in a band with all the marching, guard duty, and KP.

This sequence of events proved to me that listening to my mother, sometimes, was very sound advice.

Members of the 7th Army Symphony in 1956: (L to R) Dick Judson, Dan Reinberg, Gene Lewis, me

Army Experiences

When I hear words that make sounds, such as "whining," "moaning," "scraping," and "banging," I think back to my stint in the United States Army. All recruits in basic training took turns performing kitchen patrol, better known as KP. When my turn came, I was awakened at 4:30 a.m., reported for duty, and was instructed with another soldier to crack 100 dozen eggs into a huge vat with an outboard-type motor on the side. My colleague began whining, which was not appreciated by the mess sergeant, but I started right off with zest for a new adventure. That zest dissipated quickly after I cracked the first egg and watched as it slithered down the side into the deep cavern of the vat and slid around at the bottom, much as a cat does when circling a sunny nap spot. I looked up at the stack of full egg cartons, and heard a deep moaning sound begin down in the depths of my stomach. We did manage to finish the job, although I remember being not too particular after a while how many eggshells accompanied the eggs over the side. After breakfast our duty was to scrape all the trays of uneaten food as each soldier filed out of the mess hall. The sounds of scraping and banging of metal trays still ring in my ears.

KP would not in itself have been noteworthy, except that it made me miss a day of training. My company had spent that day learning how to "zero in your rifle," i.e., learning how to line up the sights from the middle of the rifle to the end of the barrel so that the bullets will go where you aim. This is done by rotating a small wheel next to the middle sight. A few clicks one way or the other, and the sight moves left or right. As I was absent from learning this important lesson while serving seventeen hours of KP, I was completely ignorant of how to zero my rifle.

The next day my company marched out to the rifle range and began to shoot at targets at a distance of 100 yards. I, always an eager student, asked my sergeant how to fire a rifle, something I had never done before. He said, "Just lie down, point at the target, and shoot!" I did exactly that, firing the three bullets we were given. I was rewarded with "Maggie's drawers," a red flag waving from the pit below the target, signifying that I had missed the target completely. The fellow next to me fired his three bullets, and was honored by a signal that five holes were made in his target. I had obviously shot his target twice; I had

The 7th Army Symphony bus decorated for tulip season in Holland with Jim Badger, cellist

no idea where my third bullet went. The guys on either side of me gave some well-intentioned advice about turning the little wheel to correct my aim, and I fired again. This time I had no idea where my bullets went, because the targets on either side of me registered the correct number of hits but I received "Maggie's drawers" a second time.

If I couldn't hit the target from 100 yards, the chances were slim that I would fare any better from 200 and 500 yards, and I did not. Out of 297 soldiers in my company, I came in 297th in proficiency with the M1 rifle.

My lack of success was frustrating, because I have always given the best of my ability to any task assigned. I expected to redeem myself later, when we practiced firing the bazooka; this time I was present for instruction. The drill was to kneel down and aim at a wooden tank being towed far behind a jeep, perpendicular to our line of sight. A second soldier would load the shell from behind while the first tracked the tank through a fixed sight on the side of the barrel. The loader then patted the helmet of the shooter to signal that the shell was loaded and clear to fire. Several men took their turns before me; some hit the tank and others missed. When my turn came, everything went according to plan, except that when the shell went into the barrel, I had too light a grip on the bazooka, and the weight of the shell caused the barrel to aim downward at the same time I pulled the trigger. I blew a gigantic hole about ten yards in front of me, scattering personnel in all directions. It was a good thing I was later assigned to an orchestra and not to a weapons unit!

After one year of service in the Army, all personnel were required to renew their proficiency on the rifle range. No matter what our capacity or station, we were considered soldiers first. My orders came to report to the rifle range the day before our orchestra was to leave for a month-long tour of France. My conductor sent word to my commanding officer that I would have to postpone my test for one month, but that I would take it immediately upon my return from the tour.

A month later, after completing the tour, I received notice that I had fired on the rifle range and posted a "sharpshooter" score. Puzzled, but thankful not to be humiliated again, I accepted the *fait accompli* and the sharpshooter medal that accompanied the letter. I wore that medal throughout my tour of duty, proud to be the most improved rifleman in the United States Army. Evidently, to clear the books, someone went out to the range and shot for me. I'll never know who the dead-eye was who took my place that day, nor do I care. I learned not to question the workings of the Army. It usually found one back on KP.

I was lucky to survive my Army service, not because of any combat, but because of my own ignorance. I was once charged with guarding an ammunition dump at Camp Chaffee along with a buddy. For four middle-of-the-night hours, we walked the perimeter in opposite directions. We met at a truck, where we chatted and smoked, tossing our used matches and butts onto the floor before resuming our trudge. We continued the circuit until dawn. At sunrise, to our consternation, we saw a sign in the truck next to our cigarette butts: "No smoking: This truck is full of ammo headed to the rifle range."

My First Professional Audition: The Lyric Opera, Chicago

Preparing to audition for a professional musical organization requires a great deal of courage, practice, and luck. Competing with hundreds of other candidates can devastate some of the most assured and talented musicians. They can—at the precise moment of their audition—lose their confidence and play miserably, thereby wiping out all the months of practice and preparation.

I remember well my first audition for a professional music job. It was 1956, and I was seeking to become a trumpeter in the Lyric Opera Orchestra in Chicago. Unlike auditions today, there were no set lists of music to be performed. Candidates arrived at their designated time, music was placed in front of them, and they played. One of the challenges for the candidate in advance of the audition was to guess what music might be asked of them to play, so that they might be better prepared.

My assumption was a very simple one. The Lyric Opera Orchestra was not a permanent ensemble: that year it had a season of only ten weeks. I assumed that the orchestra would have a limited library, and therefore the audition material would probably be taken from the eight operas scheduled to be performed that season. Before my audition I spent many hours in a reference library copying out all the trumpet parts from each of the eight operas. (I scratched out the notes by hand: there were no photocopiers in 1956.) At home, I practiced those opera parts for hours, until I could almost play them from memory.

When I tell this story to my students, meaning to suggest preparation methods for auditions, I get mixed reactions from them. Some say that I cheated; others admire

Playing in the Northside Symphony, a community orchestra in Chicago

my clever preparation. I tell them to study everything about the orchestra for which they are auditioning: go to a concert a few days before the audition, or hear recordings by that orchestra, and listen for the sound of the section they are attempting to join, as well as how the orchestra sounds in its hall.

In my case, I felt well prepared, so it came as a terrible shock when the orchestra contractor told me, with no explanation, that I would not be invited to audition. I was devastated! I called my former teacher Ren Schilke, who by now was retired from the Chicago Symphony but was still playing in the Lyric Opera Orchestra. He promised to find out why I was excluded. Later, he reported that my mother was the culprit. She had mentioned my audition plans to a friend of hers, who happened to live next door to the contractor. Although this friend had never heard me play, she gave the contractor a glowing report of my abilities. The contractor (reasonably) felt that if a candidate had to have his mother speak for him, he was not worth hearing. For the first time in my life I yelled at my mother, and vowed that I would never tell her of any future plans to audition. Fortunately, Ren recommended me to the contractor, who gave me a reprieve and invited me to audition.

I approached the audition full of confidence, but was completely taken aback when the first thing I was asked to play was not opera excerpts but rather a two-octave G-sharp melodic minor scale slurred up and tongued down. Having recently completed a two-year stint in the United States Army, and having ignored exotic scales since college, I stumbled badly through this assignment. I could see members of the committee fidgeting and considering dismissing me immediately. However, they were kind, and they continued, asking me to play from, yes, the opera trumpet parts. These operas were scored for the trumpeter to play in many different transpositions. I easily moved among bass, tenor, soprano, and alto clef, and read passages a step higher or a half-step lower. As I navigated the passages flawlessly, the committee forgot the mess I made of the G-sharp minor scale, and hired me on the spot for the third trumpet position. I swore I would never again be humiliated by not knowing my scales, and since then I have regularly practiced all scale variations in every possible key.

The person hired for the first trumpet position was not required to audition: he was chosen merely by his reputation as an excellent player. He was indeed superb. As the orchestra began rehearsing Verdi's *Otello* under the conductor Tullio Serafin, several glorious solo passages were sounded by the first trumpeter with a beautiful clear tone. However, later in the rehearsal the orchestra came to a long section that required the trumpet section to play in A trumpet; we had to play a minor third lower than written and add three sharps. The first trumpeter stopped playing, and his part was absent. Maestro Serafin stopped the rehearsal and, in a typical fit of rage, demanded to know what the problem was. When he discovered that the principal player could not transpose, an intermission was called to discuss the situation. The music coordinator, who had been one of the audition committee judges, suggested that I could do the job. As there was no one else available, I was appointed the new first trumpeter of the Lyric Opera Orchestra. At 25 years old I was also its youngest member. I remained with the Lyric Opera for two years before joining the Minneapolis Symphony.

With my 3 children outside our house in South Minneapolis, 1963

Members of the Minneapolis Symphony in 1960: (L to R) Jim Clute, Larry Weiman, Clem Volpe, me

Auditioning for the Minneapolis Symphony

When I heard in 1958 that the Minneapolis Symphony was holding auditions for an opening in the trumpet section, I asked my teacher, Adolph ("Bud") Herseth, if I should try for it. He replied, "By all means go up and audition. You need the experience of auditioning because it's hard to get into an orchestral position. You might as well get your feet wet!"

I flew from Chicago to Minneapolis and checked into the Sheridan Hotel, now the site of Orchestra Hall. I arrived at Northrop Auditorium, home of the Minneapolis Symphony, that afternoon and was escorted to a dressing room where I was to warm up and wait my turn to audition. In those days we were not assigned a specific time to play—all candidates showed up and sat around waiting to be called, sometimes for many hours. Also unlike modern auditions, candidates in 1958 had no idea what they would be asked to play.

I remember vividly the feeling as I waited my turn to play. The rooms on the second floor of Northrop were not soundproof, so every candidate down the long hall could be heard practicing. It was an unbelievable cacophony of sound, as each trumpeter tried to outplay the other candidates by blowing louder and higher. I heard some fantastic playing as I listened, rather than join-ing in the fray. I even entertained the notion that, given the quality of playing I heard, perhaps I should just pack up my horn, sneak out, and go home. "Oh well," I thought, "I might as well stick it out, get the experience, and then return home."

Finally I was called and ushered into the center of the auditorium's stage. I looked out at the hall, which was dark except for a few lights directly overhead on the stage. I could see what looked like a white wall at the back of the hall. The personnel manager, Jess Meltzer, a kindly and gentle man who was also a cellist in the orchestra, introduced me to principal trumpeter Bernie Adelstein. Bernie was to be the proctor on stage with me.

I don't remember what orchestral excerpt I played at first, but I do recall looking at the white wall at the back of the hall and trying to fill the auditorium with sound. The next excerpt is etched in my memory forever. Just as I began the fanfare that begins Tchaikovsky's Symphony No. 4, someone threw on the house lights—there before me was a balcony that stretched upward forever from what turned out to be a white curtain, not a back wall. I found out later that a curtain was usually drawn across the width of the auditorium to give a more intimate feeling for smaller audiences. I felt that I needed to double my output to reach the back of the hall, but the breath I had taken was inadequate for such a volume. Fortunately, Bernie was understanding, and did not count this faux pas against me.

Later that day, candidates were sitting in the green room when the person-nel manager came into the room and called several people out into the hallway. They came back in and without saying a word, packed their instruments and left. A few minutes later a few more were called out, and they too came back in and soon left quietly. Soon I was there all by myself. Jess Meltzer told me that the conductor wanted to see me. The next thing I knew, I was in the manager's office signing a contract.

I remember taking a taxi back to the airport, boarding the plane, and thanking the Lord for the opportunity to survive an audition. It wasn't until we were over Madison, Wisconsin, that it hit me. I had signed a contract to move to Minneapolis. Did I want to move to Minneapolis? I didn't know the first thing about the city. What about the orchestra—was it any good? The possibility of winning the audition hadn't even occurred to me. I had signed a contract without even talking about it to my wife!

When I got back to Chicago I called Bud Herseth. He asked how the audition had gone, and I told him, "OK, I guess—I won." "Great!" he said. "You go up there and get a few years of seasoning, and we'll get you back here in the Chicago Symphony."

In my first year the orchestra season lasted only 27 weeks. Members had other jobs during the off-season, such as selling water softeners or automobiles. I was lucky to find additional work using my horn. I played Grant Park in Chicago for 8 weeks in the summer, and band concerts at Lake Harriet in Minneapolis. In 1961 I started teaching lessons at St. Olaf College, and the following year at the University of Minnesota.

The local paper welcomes new members of the Minneapolis Symphony

The years went by. I had two children by 1959. Minneapolis became much more appealing as the symphony season gradually added more weeks, and the weekly salary rose from $110 in 1958 to $150 in 1961. Major league sports teams, the Twins and Vikings, arrived in town (although we lost the Lakers to Los Angeles). Returning to Chicago for family visits gave us a chance to evaluate the differences in the cities. When I compared neighborhoods I could afford to live in and overall quality of life, Minneapolis won hands down. I never seriously considered moving back to Chicago.

Brass players in the Minneapolis Symphony: (back row L to R) Larry Weiman, Steve Zellmer, Steve Chenette, Clem Volpe, me, (front row) Ron Ricketts, Frank Winsor, Bob Ellworthy

Now That I Won the Audition—

In my first concert as a new member of the Minneapolis Symphony, I had to come on from backstage and walk past the timpani and three other trumpet players to take my place as fourth trumpet. As I wiggled past the percussion section, my fly caught on the timpani's tuning pegs and spread open the buttons of my pants. I tried to cover my fly as I squeezed down the row of players, in full view of the entire audience. So this is what it's like to be a professional musician!

I nearly lost my job during my first tour, thanks to Debussy's *La Mer*. This piece is a bane of trumpet players: we sit for 17 minutes, then enter on a solo part, very high and soft, diminishing to nothing. The orchestra took *La Mer* on tour when I was still wet behind the ears and unfamiliar with the standard repertoire. In the middle of a concert in Edmonton, Alberta, Jim Greco, who was to play the solo part, said "Here, young fellow, you need experience. Let's switch parts for the Debussy." Not knowing any better, I said "Sure." I sat for 17 minutes while the rest of the orchestra played. I came in fine on my first note but, not realizing that it was supposed to be a solo, I thought I must have miscounted, and I stopped playing. Conductor Antal Dorati was furious. He conducted the rest of the piece glaring at me. I thought I was done in the orchestra. One of the bass players behind me told me after the concert that Greco switched with me because he never played the passage correctly.

On my first tour to Carnegie Hall, the Cleveland Orchestra played a rehearsal in the hall during the afternoon. I ducked in to hear, and I was the only one in the whole hall. At one point George Szell turned around to the hall and asked, "How is the balance between the clarinet and the cellos?" I replied "Fine!" The orchestra members burst into laughter. Unbeknownst to me, the associate conductor had come into the hall and was sitting behind me. George Szell would never have asked an unknown kid like me how his balance was.

Postscript to *La Mer:* much later, after I retired from the orchestra, I had occasion to call a former violinist, Francis Thevenin. I wanted to invite him to a photo op that the orchestra was staging of former veterans. We chatted, and he said "Ron, you know what I remember most about you? You never missed the *La Mer* part."

Playing an extracurricular gig with Fred Keller and Jim Greco

Guthrie Theater musicians in the 1960s: (back row, L to R) Dave Karr, Warren Alm, Marv Dahlgren, (front row) Jack Coan, Herb Pilhofer, me

Déjà Vu: Herald Trumpets

One of my first opportunities to play trumpet professionally came in 1953, when a touring company of the Metropolitan Opera presented a performance of Verdi's *Aida* in Chicago. My friend Tom Crown, two others, and I were contracted to play herald trumpets for the performance. We were to play standing on a ledge above the rear of the main stage during the scene when Radames leads a triumphal procession after defeating the Ethiopians.

A regular member of the Met trumpet section, Izzy Blank, traveled with the company and supervised the local musicians. He had us practice on the herald trumpets, which are normal B-flat instruments but laid out in a straight line approximately 30 inches long. Once we rehearsed and memorized the fanfare, we were outfitted with heavy Egyptian-style robes with long sleeves and tall Egyptian headgear. There was no dress rehearsal; in costume, we were told at the performance to follow Izzy up the ladder and onto the ledge. When he raised his trumpet, we were to do likewise and follow the conductor below in the orchestra pit. We did as instructed, and were pleased with ourselves after the show. We heard nothing but praise for our fanfare.

However, Claudia Cassidy, music critic for the *Chicago Tribune,* was not as impressed. In an otherwise glowing review of the performance, she wrote, "I don't believe gold wrist watches and glasses were worn by Egyptian trumpeters during the epoch of the Pharaohs!" Tom and I had both worn our glasses on stage, so as to see the conductor, and when we raised our trumpets to play, our sleeves slid down to our elbows, revealing our watches. My first significant professional gig, and I got mentioned in the *Tribune,* but fortunately not by name!

Me, Jeff Tyzik, Doc Severinsen, Allen Vizzutti, Mike Hipps, Steve Wright

Eleven years later, in 1964, I was living in Minneapolis. Dan Tetzlaff, a friend, fellow trumpet player, and schoolteacher, was one of five musicians on staff at the newly opened Guthrie Theater. Wednesday matinee performances conflicted with Dan's school schedule, so I was invited to sub for him playing fanfares on the Guthrie's herald trumpets. The theater used live fanfares from a little balcony to alert audiences that performances were about to begin and that intermissions were coming to an end.

My first matinee was a performance of Shakespeare's *Hamlet,* a play that required one fanfare on stage during the second act in addition to the lobby calls. Jack Coan, Warren Alm, and I were the trumpeters, and Marv Dahlgren was the percussionist. Before the show we practiced the fanfares on the herald trumpets until I had them memorized. The regular trumpeters told me that I should follow Jack up the ladder and out over the stage to a small balcony. When a little blue light in the back of the hall flickered and went out, I should raise the horn and play the fanfare. It sounded simple, but I had the feeling that I had traveled this route before. Déjà vu? At the right time, I followed Jack out onto the balcony, which had a metal railing along the bottom, 15 inches high. I stood perfectly still, eyes glued on the blue light. When the light went out, the other two trumpeters lifted their horns straight up for a few inches to clear the railing, then swung them parallel to the floor. I, however, pivoted my horn up, catching the bell on the rim of the railing. The bell made a sound like a crashing cymbal and began to vibrate, making it nearly impossible to position my lips on the mouthpiece. Out of the corner of my eye I could see the actors jerking their heads in concert to look up at me.

I don't know if it is the herald trumpets themselves or the theater setting that inspires my fear, but I will decline any future offers to play them. Déjà vu!

"Amazing Grace" on fluegelhorn for the funeral of a beloved family member

At 11 years old, earning second prize in the Morris B. Sachs Amateur Hour with Vander Cook's "Lily Polka"

Early Teachers

For better or worse, I can recall only one teacher from my first eight years of classroom schooling. It was 1940, and I was in the second grade. I clearly remember the events of that year because Germany was overrunning Europe and Africa. In school, when we went out for recess, my teacher would stand at the top of the stairs and pound out a heavy cadence on the railing with her ruler. We would march in time down the stairs and out to the playground. I often thought many years later that she was probably a secret Nazi, enamored of the Hitler Youth movement, and was training us to become a regiment of storm troopers.

My other, and more vivid, recollection of this same teacher occurred at the beginning of the school year, when she asked us to draw a picture of something we did or saw the previous summer. With great anticipation I took out my black, white, and red crayons to draw a picture of an airplane on the construction paper. My mother had taken my sister and me out to Midway Airport in Chicago late one afternoon to watch the planes take off and land. The planes at the airport that day were all single- or two-engine propeller planes. After dinner we learned that a four-engine airplane was due to land around midnight. A great deal of whining ensued, I'm sure mainly by me, and Mom agreed to wait. When that plane came in, it was the most beautiful sight I had ever seen! It taxied directly toward the terminal then turned to the right and stopped directly in front of the window where we were standing. The floodlights of the terminal shone brightly on the side of the plane, and I saw a sleek white body with huge letters "TWA" painted on the side.

My euphoric state returned in that classroom as I began to draw a picture of the airplane that I so graphically visualized in my mind's eye. When I finished drawing I proudly walked to the front of the room to turn in my masterpiece. I was shocked when the teacher began to shake her head and said that my picture was all wrong. I said, "That's what I saw!" But she insisted, "There is no such word as TWA—it had to be TWO." Brooking no argument, she marked a C on my drawing. I'm sure she had never seen an airplane up close or ridden in one. Of course, I didn't know then that TWA stood for Trans World Airlines; if I had known, I might have made a stand. I think back to that episode in context of my later shyness and reluctance to answer questions in class for fear that my classmates would laugh at me whether my answer was right or not.

I remember my first trumpet teacher, Mr. Berenger, only because he sat between a beginning saxophone student and me on cornet. I never understood why we had to take lessons together, but at nine years of age, one doesn't ask too many questions. I assume now that it was hard to find someone to give me individual cornet lessons that cost only one dollar per lesson.

I liked my next cornet teacher, Sam Conti, because he owned a hobby store. I had my lessons in the back of the store, then would get a ten-cent block of balsa wood to take home after the lesson and carve into a model airplane. Mr. Conti was also a fine professional trumpet player. I remember going to downtown Chicago with my mother to hear him play in the pit orchestra of the Broadway show *Oklahoma!* at the Shubert Theater. It gave me a great sense of pride when, thirteen years later, I played a three-month engagement in the same pit, playing the Broadway show *My Fair Lady.*

William Hebs was my next cornet teacher. He lived in the far north part of Chicago, requiring me to ride three streetcars to reach his home. Two important events bring those days quickly to my memory. One day, several hours before my scheduled lesson, a P-51 Mustang fighter plane crashed into the back of an apartment building about a mile from my house. My buddy Wes and I were playing in my backyard and had watched this plane flying stunt maneuvers over my house; then we saw it trail smoke and go into a dive. We quickly mounted our bicycles and headed off to the site, arriving before the fire engines. (Living in an industrial area of Chicago, we always had our bicycles facing out at a ready position because fires were frequent, and we were self-appointed junior firemen.) The carnage was terrible, as the plane had clipped the top of a garage and slammed into the side of the apartment building, setting all three stories on fire.

The point of this story for me is that after a couple of hours watching the firemen battle the blaze, I remembered my scheduled cornet lesson. I hurried home on my bicycle, got cleaned up, and went to my lesson. I have often wondered, for me to have left all that excitement, was I in a state of shock over what I had witnessed, or was my dedication to the trumpet already that strong?

The second recollection I have of my lessons with Mr. Hebs came after the end of an excellent lesson. I had played all my exercises and etudes well, and I had played higher notes than ever before. But after the lesson, as I walked in a euphoric state down the long flight of stairs in front of his house and three houses down the street, I heard a pleading call from his house, "Ronald, Ronald, did you forget to pay me?" I was embarrassed to have forgotten to pay Mr. Hebs, but more important, I felt sorry for the feeble cry from a man who needed his two dollars. I vowed then that if I ever became a private trumpet instructor, I would never ask a student for the money if he forgot to pay me. Today I would be willing to bet that of the thousands of lessons I have taught throughout my career, I probably lost three fees. To me, that is a small price to pay to banish the image of that man standing at the top of the stairs, pitifully calling my name.

For a time I took lessons from Ralph Martiere, a WGN studio trumpet player. He later had a big band that won the *DownBeat* poll for big bands. When I arrived for a lesson one Sunday after church, his wife Edith sent me up to get him out of bed. He came downstairs and sat in a corner in his bathrobe smoking a cigarette with a plastic filter holder. A publisher had sent him a perusal copy of bop duets, which we tried playing together. He threw the music into a trash basket with expletives about how terrible bop music was. I retrieved the duet book (with his permission) and kept it. Fifteen years later I brought it out to sight-read with one of my students and discovered how delightful these duets were. My taste in music had matured!

Now that I am the teacher, I sometimes wonder what my students take away from their lessons. I always encourage students to practice scales for five minutes every day. Once I was writing out some scales for a student, and he said, "You should have been a doctor." "Why?" "I can't read what you are writing."

Pausing in the backyard from photographing everyone else

For many years, I was never far from my horn

Carnegie Hall

What is the mystique evoked whenever the name "Carnegie Hall" is uttered? Is Carnegie Hall a place where things happen that are not possible anywhere else? Are the people who enter there transformed into some new dimension? Are the performers super-musicians?

It could be all of the above, yet I think not. Carnegie Hall has been in the forefront of the musical world simply because over the years it has premiered more compositions, orchestras, soloists, and conductors than any other concert hall in the world. Orchestras and soloists from everywhere make their reputations once they are acclaimed by critics for the *New York Times* or *Herald*. Stardom is theirs if they receive a glowing review of their performance the night before. In Europe, performers are considered provincial until they have proven themselves in concert halls such as Musikverein in Vienna, Barbican Centre in

London, and Théâtre des Champs-Élysées in Paris. Carnegie is such a proving ground for musicians from all over the world.

I remember as a child listening to the Sunday broadcaster say, "And now we bring to you live, from Carnegie Hall, the New York Philharmonic under the direction of Dimitri Mitropoulos." Most of my school friends were outside playing kick the can on the street in front of my house, but I was glued to the radio. There I was introduced to the likes of Beethoven, Mozart, Brahms, and many other composers whose names I could not then pronounce. Little did I know at that time that many years later I would be on that same stage, playing my trumpet in an orchestra being broadcast throughout the United States and to Europe.

I can still remember the thrill when I first walked into Carnegie Hall over fifty years ago. The Minneapolis Symphony had been on tour for two weeks throughout the eastern United States, playing mostly in college auditoriums, gymnasiums, and movie theaters. I could feel the excitement growing each night as we played our con-

With Bea and Midori in 2002

certs and the date for New York City came nearer. As the day approached, I could hear people practicing their instruments more fervently throughout the hotels.

Finally the day arrived. We checked into the Great Northern Hotel on 56th Street, a few blocks from Carnegie Hall. I couldn't wait to see the shrine that I had been dreaming about for so long. Clem Volpe and I went immediately to the stage door. We were confronted by a big, burly guard who demanded to know who we were. We meekly showed him our credentials, and he reluctantly let us pass.

We found our instrument trunks, took out our horns, and sought a corner of the hall to warm up. I was not shy: I walked right out onto center stage, and stood there spellbound. Here is where all the great musicians had performed! Here is where Tchaikovsky conducted his own works, as had Stravinsky, Richard

Strauss, Copland, and countless others. This is where Bernstein, Mitropoulos, Ormandy, Toscanini, and many other great conductors had led the New York Philharmonic.

I began to play. Suddenly I sensed the presence of past performers all around me. I was playing for them! I was playing a solo on the stage of Carnegie Hall! As I played, I looked way up, to the top balcony. The uppermost row of the balcony rose almost straight up above me. The first ring of balcony seats appeared to encircle the stage and hold me. I was in heaven! Now I needed to see what the audience would view of the stage from their seats, so I wandered through the hall and up to the top balcony. The view of the stage, so far away, was breathtaking. One of my fellow musicians appeared on stage; he seemed so tiny from that distance.

Backstage was a crowded room where our instruments and dressing trunks were placed. By evening, when all the musicians arrived for the concert, we were jammed into that room, trying to change into our concert dress and to open our instrument trunks.

I don't remember the pieces we played the first time I appeared on that stage; I remember only the feeling of being present. I estimate that I played Carnegie thirty-eight times during my career, and I felt the same excitement each time.

The hallway leading to the Carnegie stage features photographs of visiting orchestras. Every time we toured to New York, I looked in vain for a picture of our orchestra under either name, Minneapolis Symphony or Minnesota Orchestra. It seemed that every orchestra but ours was honored with a picture on the wall. Finally, about three years before I retired, Manny Laureano drew a stick picture of the Minnesota Orchestra and taped it to the wall. The next time we played there, we found a beautiful photo of us placed prominently in the hallway.

The old familiar story goes, "Hey buddy, can you tell me how to get to Carnegie Hall?" "Practice, practice, practice." The adage will always ring true. I'm glad I practiced, for I fulfilled my lifelong dream.

Conductor Osmo Vänskä with four former personnel managers, spanning 25 years of service: Heather Larson, Julie Haight, me, Brian Woods

Auditions for the Minnesota Orchestra: From the Other Side

Have you ever wondered how the musicians in a professional group such as the Minnesota Orchestra get their jobs? The answer: by audition. When an opening occurs, the management places an ad in newspapers and the standard trade magazines that circulate throughout the world. Musicians who want to audition write to the personnel manager of the orchestra to submit their résumé and express their interest.

I. Invitation to Audition

Audition committees at the Minnesota Orchestra are comprised of current orchestra members. The committees establish the details of the audition process, subject to the approval of management. If a candidate's credentials are strong, or if the committee is familiar with the candidate's playing ability, the committee extends an invitation to participate in live auditions. Other candidates must submit a recording of their playing, which is evaluated by the committee; if the recording is approved, the candidate is invited to the live audition.

Once a list of candidates has been established, those on the list are sent information about the date, time, and place of the audition. They are also sent a list of the required repertoire, usually one or two solos and a selection of orchestral excerpts that display a player's tone, technique, musicianship, and general command of the instrument.

II. Preliminary Round

When candidates arrive at the hall on the appointed day, they are met by the personnel manager's assistant, who assigns them to a warm-up room, usually 45 minutes to an hour before the audition time. The assistant keeps candidates informed if the auditions are running behind or ahead of schedule. At ten minutes before they are scheduled to play, the associate personnel manager tells them which solo they are to play and which excerpts. The manager also advises candidates on the physical set-up of the hall, its acoustics, its shape, placement of any screen, and where in the hall the committee is seated. The manager makes any other appropriate suggestions, such as asking women to remove heeled shoes that would click on the floor and telegraph their gender. Candidates are encouraged to play a few notes on stage before the audition begins, to test the acoustics and liveliness of the hall.

At Orchestra Hall, auditions are held on the stage. To ensure that all candidates remain anonymous, the committee sits behind a screen that is placed 15 rows back from the stage. Candidates are assigned a number, and are never referred to by name or gender, even by staff members working backstage. A proctor—usually the personnel manager—is also on stage to aid the candidates with any whispered questions they may want to ask. A typical preliminary audition lasts from ten to fifteen minutes.

After the audition, candidates are invited to wait in the musicians' lounge while the committee hears more candidates and decides whether to pass any on to the next round of auditions. The committee usually hears five candidates in a single session, and then deliberates and votes on those five. They present their decision to the personnel manager, who relays it to the waiting candidates.

Sitting backstage in the lounge is the most difficult time of the audition, as candidates begin to relax and mentally replay the performance they just completed. Unsuccessful candidates often have a clear idea why they were not advanced to the next round; most say that nerves kept them from doing their best. When brass players are nervous, their mouths go dry and they cannot slur or tongue with ease, even though glasses of water are provided on stage during their audition. String players' nerves make their hands sweaty and their vibrato uneven.

III. The Semifinal Round

Eight or nine candidates survive the preliminary round and move on to a semi-final round, for which a different solo and new orchestral excerpts are selected. Because this stage is more critical than the preliminary audition, members of the committee might ask a candidate to play a passage again to see whether they can correct it or make it more musical. The committee thereby learns how quickly a candidate can adapt to change, a necessary requirement given the orchestra's fast rehearsal pace.

IV. The Final Round

Three or four candidates move on to the final round. If any candidate is presently playing in the orchestra (for example, if a section player is auditioning for a principal position), this round is also held behind a screen to ensure fairness. If the candidates are all from outside the orchestra, the screen comes down, candidates are referred to by name instead of by number, and candidates' résumés are distributed to the committee.

The final round is the only part of the audition that the music director attends. This round is more comprehensive than the previous stages, with more excerpts and more comments from the committee and the conductor. The music director may conduct candidates to see how carefully they follow his direction. Candidates might be asked to play passages in ensemble with members of the committee. If the audition is for a woodwind or brass position, they may play in a sectional with similar instruments; for a string opening, they may play in a quartet. Ensemble playing often reveals how well candidates will blend into the section for which they are auditioning.

After all the scheduled playing has taken place, a secret ballot is taken by the committee before any discussion of the candidates occurs. The ballots are tallied by the personnel managers, and the results are relayed to the music director and the committee. One by one, committee members offer their opinions about the strengths and weaknesses of each finalist. The conductor listens to all members, then gives his appraisal of the finalists. If all agree, the audition is over. If no clear majority is forthcoming, one or two candidates may be asked to play again, and are told what they need to correct in their playing. Those not in the running by this time are released.

After more playing, another secret vote is taken. Then there is more discussion, followed by another vote. If doubt lingers in the committee about an individual finalist, the candidate may be asked to return at a later date to play in the orchestra for a few weeks as a continuation of the audition process. This gives musicians sitting around the candidate an opportunity to carefully evaluate their playing. After the term of temporary membership, a vote is taken by the section involved as well as the audition committee. If the vote is "Yea," the finalist is accepted into the orchestra. If the vote is "No," the whole audition process begins again, with the placing of an advertisement!

The entire audition, from initial announcement to final decision, usually lasts six months. Live auditions can take three full days, often from 9 a.m. to 10 p.m. It is a long and arduous process, but it ensures that vacancies are carefully and impartially filled with only the most qualified performers. This is the procedure that keeps the Minnesota Orchestra in the forefront of the symphony world.

The Minnesota Orchestra Brass Quintet: (L to R) Clem Volpe, Bob Ellworthy, Ron Ricketts, Steve Zellmer, me

Orchestra Hall Groundbreaking

It was a bright, warm, and beautiful day in downtown Minneapolis for the groundbreaking of the new Orchestra Hall in 1974. All the dignitaries were present with their gold construction helmets and shovels: conductor Stanislaw Skrowaczewski; many orchestra staff members; board members, including chair John Meyers; and TV news, radio, and newspaper reporters and cameramen. The Minnesota Brass Quintet, in which I played principal trumpet, was asked to perform preliminary music before the 12:30 p.m. festivities.

I observed something that had apparently gone otherwise unnoticed. The dignitaries were ready to push the first groundbreaking shovels into . . . what? The parking lot we occupied was solid asphalt. I motioned to John Meyers the obvious folly about to unfold. He slapped his forehead and somehow was able to telephone for a truckload of dirt to be quickly delivered. The truck arrived while our quintet was playing and dumped an entire load of dirt right next to us, covering some of our shoes. I felt like a child playing in a sandbox.

The dirt dump was not mentioned in any of the news media, but it is my most vivid memory of the new hall. A photograph from a nearby office tower shows the pile of dirt remaining at the building site after the festivities were over.

The future site of Orchestra Hall, including dirt imported for the groundbreaking ceremony

Minneapolis Symphony Orchestra
1913 Spring Tour

Emil Oberhoffer, Conductor

SOLOISTS:

Luella Chilson-Ohrman, Soprano
Barbara Wait, Contralto
Joseph Schenke, Tenor
Arthur Middleton, Baritone
Richard Czerwonky, Violin
Cornelius van Vliet, Cello
Henry J. Williams, Harp

* Dates with both afternoon and evening concerts.

April 6	Minneapolis, Minnesota
April 7 *	Winnipeg, Manitoba
April 8 *	Winnipeg, Manitoba
April 9 *	Winnipeg, Manitoba
April 10 *	Brandon, Manitoba
April 11 *	Devils Lake, North Dakota
April 12 *	Grand Forks, North Dakota
April 13	Litchfield, Minnesota
April 14	Northfield, Minnesota
April 15 *	Northfield, Minnesota
April 16 *	Des Moines, Iowa
April 17 *	Des Moines, Iowa
April 18 *	Kirksville, Missouri
April 19 *	Kirksville, Missouri
April 20	St. Joseph, Missouri
April 21 *	Atchison, Kansas
April 22 *	Leavenworth, Kansas
April 23 *	Tulsa, Oklahoma

April 24 *	Springfield, Missouri
April 25 *	Lawrence, Kansas
April 26 *	Hutchinson, Kansas
April 27	Sunday off
April 28 *	Wichita, Kansas
April 29 *	Columbia, Missouri
April 30	Evansville, Indiana
May 1 *	Evansville, Indiana
May 2	Charleston, Illinois
May 2	Terre Haute, Indiana
May 3 *	Greencastle, Indiana
May 4	Sunday off
May 5 *	Indianapolis, Indiana
May 6	Akron, Ohio
May 7 *	Akron, Ohio
May 8 *	Kalamazoo, Michigan
May 9 *	South Bend, Indiana
May 10 *	Valparaiso, Indiana
May 11	Sunday off
May 12	Appleton, Wisconsin
May 13 *	Appleton, Wisconsin
May 14 *	Benton Harbor, Michigan
May 15 *	Lafayette, Indiana
May 16 *	Bloomington, Illinois
May 17 *	Decatur, Illinois
May 18	Peoria, Illinois
May 19	Monmouth, Illinois
May 19	Burlington, Iowa
May 20 *	Galesburg, Illinois
May 21 *	Moline, Illinois
May 22	Cedar Rapids, Iowa
May 23 *	Cedar Rapids, Iowa
May 24 *	Cedar Rapids, Iowa
May 25	Sunday off

May 26 *	Oskaloosa, Iowa
May 27	Lincoln, Nebraska
May 27	Omaha, Nebraska
May 28 *	Grand Island, Nebraska
May 29 *	Sioux City, Iowa
May 30 *	Mitchell, South Dakota
May 31 *	Sioux Falls, South Dakota
June 1 *	Aberdeen, South Dakota
June 2 *	Aberdeen, South Dakota
June 3 *	Valley City, North Dakota
June 4 *	Grand Forks, North Dakota
June 5	Pending
June 6	Pending
June 7	Pending

The Minnesota Orchestra trumpet section in 1998: Bob Dorer, Manny Laureano, me, Mike Hipps

Orchestra on Wheels

This is a story about a life filled with recognition, sacrifices, humor, and lasting friendships: a life as a member of a touring professional orchestra. "Orchestra on wheels" describes the Minneapolis Symphony during its early years, as the orchestra was commonly on the road for four or five weeks at a time, and often toured multiple times in a single season. One of the orchestra's early tours, led by conductor Emil Oberhoffer, began on April 6, 1913, en route to Winnipeg, Manitoba; that tour ended on June 7 in Grand Forks, North Dakota, nine weeks later. Between those dates the orchestra played 103 concerts in Minnesota, Manitoba, North Dakota, Iowa, Missouri, Kansas, Oklahoma, Indiana, Illinois, Ohio, Michigan, Wisconsin, Nebraska, and South Dakota. The 60-day tour included 47 cities, most with both an afternoon and an evening concert, with only four free days.

When I joined the Minneapolis Symphony in 1958 under Antal Dorati, the orchestra season was 27 weeks long. The other 25 weeks of the year I played dance jobs, taught trumpet lessons, and played in the Grant Park orchestra in Chicago. Of the Minneapolis Symphony's 27 regular-season weeks that year, we toured nine of them, all by bus; this amounted to one-third of the season on the road. We played 42 concerts throughout Florida, Alabama, South Carolina, North Carolina, Georgia, Virginia, Tennessee, Wisconsin, Iowa, Illinois, Indiana, and Minnesota.

Being with one's colleagues sixteen hours a day for weeks at a time took its toll on one's demeanor. There was a saying in our orchestra, "If you were friends at the end of a four- or five-week tour, you were friends for life." Being part of a touring orchestra also meant that we had to make sacrifices. My daughter Laurie was born in Florida when the orchestra was playing in Clemson, South Carolina. When I requested permission to take a weekend leave of absence to go see her, the general manager said to me, "Do you want this job or not, *kid?*" That tour encompassed 28 concerts in 32 days and 11 states; we were home for only 12 days before departing again on a three-week Midwestern tour. I didn't see my baby daughter for the first time until she was two months old! My other daughter, Judy, was born in Minneapolis when we were on tour in Tallahassee, Florida. I received the same response from the manager and didn't see her until she was one month old.

Because the orchestra played most of its concerts in small towns, the musicians were housed in motels, which ranged in quality from A (the best) to B and C (lower-grade accommodations). The first-chair players and senior members of the orchestra stayed in the A motels, while the section players and newer members were relegated to the B and C motels. Sending mail to touring musicians was difficult during this period, as motel assignments were not posted until our arrival in the town. To counter this obstacle, I volunteered to be Postmaster (no one else wanted the job) with the duty of retrieving the mail at General Delivery and distributing it to the members. For this honor I received a bonus of $10 a week and a free taxi ride to and from the center of town to pick up the mail. This helped my popularity with fellow musicians, who tagged along for a free ride.

The bus drivers weren't always the professionals we hoped they would be. In Washington, D.C., the bus driver got lost. So we called a cab, gave the driver our destination, and the bus followed the cab to our hotel. On our way to the College of St. Benedict, in St. Peter, Minnesota, we decided that our smallish orchestra didn't need both buses that we had ordered, so we sent one back. The second bus driver had apparently been told to follow the first, so the orchestra ended up at the bus garage.

When the full orchestra went on in-state tours we often needed three buses. One bus was for smokers, one was for nonsmokers, and one was half and half. The smokers dubbed the nonsmoking bus the "hospital bus."

During the 1960s we began to travel less by bus and more by train, with our own separate sleeping cars. As the train pulled into a station, the orchestra cars were disconnected and placed on a siding off from the main track; the rest of the train continued on its regularly scheduled run. We spent the day walking around town, seeing a movie, or playing basketball at the local YMCA. After

Traveling in style

dinner we played a concert and retreated to our train cars, where we played cards or just relaxed. Sometime during the night another train would pull into the station, hitch up our cars, and travel to the next town, where the procedure would be repeated day after day until we reached the West Coast. Once, on a steam train, Frank Winsor (horn) and I stood on the outdoor platform of the last car to catch some air. We enjoyed the thrill of blackness as the train went through a tunnel. Later, when we went inside the train, everybody burst out laughing. The soot from the train had covered our faces while we were in the tunnel.

In later years we traveled by train but stayed in hotels. This created a new set of difficulties, for the orchestra did not furnish buses. When we exited the train in a new town we had to find the means of getting to our hotel by ourselves. Our per diem allowance was $11, out of which we had to pay for meals, hotels, and taxis. We decided in each town whether to walk the one or two miles to the hotel in order to save our per diem, carrying our suitcases and instruments, or wait with 100 other people for the few taxis. When we did take taxis, we typically found only three cabs at the train station. We'd have to wait our turn for these three vehicles to make the run and return.

The hotels, too, were frequently disappointing. One hotel room in LaCrosse, Wisconsin, was furnished with only a bed, a bare light bulb, and one straight-backed chair. The toilet facilities were down the hall, shared by eight rooms. The hotel had only one black-and-white television set, in the lobby. If we newbies wanted to watch TV, we had to stand behind older members who sat in the lobby for hours during the day, smoking and carving pipes.

For the evening concerts, our tour manager Glenn Cooke would charter one city bus for the entire orchestra to ride to the concert. He would stand outside the bus with a coin changer and charge us twenty-five cents for the privilege of being jammed in a bus with ninety-seven colleagues. I remember once being by the back door of the bus, crushed up against the glass so tightly that the door could not be opened until everyone in front moved off the bus.

Modesty was frequently absent on these tours, perhaps as a carryover from the days when orchestra personnel were all male. Many times we had only one dressing room, and the seven women changed their clothes right next to the men. The clothing was less impressive in the early days than it is today: without wash-and-wear, and often without time to visit a laundromat, we would sometimes wash our clothes in the hotel sink and hang them to dry all over the room, from lamps, window blinds, and moldings. When the white shirts got dirty, some musicians put powder on the collars to cover gray areas.

Glenn seemed to improvise on some of our travel arrangements. Occasionally I saw him studying train schedules during our concerts. Once after a concert we boarded buses, drove for an hour, and disembarked on a lonely road that crossed a railroad track. We waited for forty-five minutes in the dark, standing along a single track; a train stopped, we boarded, and we traveled to the next town.

Touring did have its humorous moments. One night around midnight when we pulled into a station, one of our violinists asked the train conductor if he had time to go into the station for a sandwich. The conductor, who was more than a little amused to see a musician in pajamas and robe, said, "Yes, but be advised that part of this train is being temporarily placed on a siding while another train pulls in here. You have about thirty minutes." A few minutes later, the orchestra cars were pulled out and another train pulled in. The violinist was aware of all this switching back and forth, but not too concerned, as he relished his midnight snack in the station. After he finished his sandwich he boarded a train car where he thought he had exited, and as the train left the station he walked down the aisle looking for his berth. He kept walking until he came to the coal car at one end of the train and the lounge car at the other. The realization suddenly dawned on him that he had boarded the wrong train, and was traveling in the opposite direction from the orchestra. The next stop for this train was fifty miles away, where he exited that train and purchased a ticket for the orchestra's destination. Boarding another train the next morning, he sat with the morning commuters while wearing his pajamas and robe. This event has been told and retold for many years throughout the orchestral community, and has brought smiles as well as dread to many touring musicians: "May something like this never happen to me."

Another memorable event occurred on our way to play a concert in Lancaster, Pennsylvania. A month after the Three Mile Island nuclear meltdown, our tour required the buses to travel past the disaster site. Twenty-seven musicians, fearing contamination, refused to ride those buses. They chartered their own bus and took a wide detour that caused them to miss the concert. Our management filled the vacancies with substitutes from a nearby music conservatory.

A shocking blast to my gut occurred on a day off from a southern tour, when I had taken the free day in South Carolina to visit my pregnant wife and young son, who were waiting out the tour with my in-laws in Florida. To return to the orchestra I had to catch a midnight bus. When I walked into the Greyhound station, a pleasant-looking black woman came up to me and said, "Sir I don't thinks you wants to wait in here. This room is for colored folks. The white waiting room is next door." I was stunned. In 1959, such division didn't exist in my world. As I walked out I passed two drinking fountains side by side, one labeled "for colored" and the other "white." After growing up in Chicago and spending two years in the Army, I had forgotten that such racial segregation existed in the United States.

One of my friends in the orchestra was a dark-skinned man from South

Asia. In some southern states on those early tours, he was able to accompany us to dinner only after he donned a turban.

We endured many harrowing tour experiences throughout the years, from blizzards and landslides to flooded bridges and automobile accidents. But somehow we rarely missed a concert.

Present-day touring with the Minnesota Orchestra has attained the character of a first-class vacation. Suitcases are loaded onto buses at Orchestra Hall and transferred by baggage handlers onto airplanes, onto buses, and into our hotel rooms. The only time players carry their own luggage is to go through customs. The hotels are the finest available. The concert halls are the most elegant in Europe, Japan, and the United States. Comfortable coach buses are chartered to take the musicians from the hotel to the concert hall, even if it is only a few blocks away, and the musicians are not charged twenty-five cents to ride! I'm glad that I was a part of the old "orchestra on wheels," because it helped me appreciate how wonderful touring became near the end of my career.

All Star Quintet in Carmel, California, 1995: (L to R) me, Warren Deck, Glenn Dodson, Charlie Schlueter, Phil Myers

Roger Sessions and Modern Music

For the 1959–1960 season, Antal Dorati and the Minneapolis Symphony commissioned Roger Sessions to write his Symphony No. 4. On January 2, 1960, the orchestra played its third rehearsal of the new symphony, with Sessions pacing behind the orchestra smoking a pipe. The personnel manager whispered to Dorati that our first trumpet player, Bernie Adelstein, would be late because snowplows had buried his driveway after the morning's snowstorm. Dorati told me to move over from the third trumpet chair and cover the first part until Bernie could get to the hall.

I took Bernie's spot and picked up the first trumpet part, and we began to play the third movement. About fifteen minutes in, Dorati asked me to play more lyrically. He looked to Sessions for confirmation, and Sessions, with pipe still in his mouth, muttered that yes, more lyrical would be fine. A few minutes later, Dorati asked me to play more "bravura" on a particular passage, and Sessions again concurred.

After an hour had passed, I noticed Bernie standing offstage looking in, so

I motioned for him to come take over, but he shook his head; he mimed that he wanted to warm up first, then take over after intermission, in about fifteen minutes.

When intermission was called, Bernie came over, put his hand on my shoulder, and said, "Good job, Ron. But if you get to play it again, the part is in B-flat, not C." I had played the entire symphony a whole step higher than written, and none of us had noticed my error, not even the conductor or the composer. This after two and a half rehearsals!

Looking back over the program, I see that the rest of the program called for trumpets in C and D:

Barbirolli, *Elizabethan Suite in C* (Trumpet in C)

De Falla, Three dances from the ballet *Three-Cornered Hat*
    (Trumpet in C)

Brahms, Concerto for Piano with Claudio Arrau (Trumpet in D)

This is not offered as an excuse on my part: I should have looked at the first page of the trumpet part before I began to play. Nevertheless, I indignantly felt that both Sessions and Dorati should have known better.

A Hasselmann family picnic: (standing, from L) cousin Rollie, mother Evelyn, me, sister Jean, cousin Georgie, aunt Vernetta, (seated) uncles Harry, Al, and Ray, aunt Olivia, uncle George

We're Proud of You, Ronnie

My Uncle George, Aunt Olivia, cousin Georgie, and Georgie's wife Barb came to visit us from Chicago one year. They asked to see where I worked, so I gave them a tour of Orchestra Hall, including the backstage area, my personnel office, pictures of many famous people on the walls, and out onto the stage to visualize how the players see the audience. They moved down the stairs and took seats about 10 rows back from the stage. They asked me to get my trumpet and play something so they could sense the sound in the hall. I did, and played some orchestral excerpts. Then my uncle asked me to play the "Star-Spangled Banner." As I played, I was aware of doors opening all over the upper balconies where staff offices were located, as people wondered what was going on below. To my astonishment, my family rose from their seats and placed their hands over their hearts. I nearly cried, I was so proud of them.

My sister Jean and her husband Norm came to Minneapolis for a visit. Norm watched my trumpet students come in and out of the house, taking their lessons and paying me afterward. He joked to some of his friends about how his brother-in-law in Minneapolis had such a great racket, with kids coming to his house, spending some time downstairs, and giving him money. On a subsequent visit, Norm slept in late while I taught several lessons. He was sitting at the kitchen table having a cup of coffee and reading the newspaper when the doorbell rang; it was a student returning to the house after forgetting to pay me. This student handed Norm a check and said, "Would you give this to Mr. Hasselmann? It's for my lesson." This was too much for Norm. Now he told his friends, "They come to the door and just hand over the money without even taking their lesson! What a racket!"

My paternal grandmother (center), father (standing, second from left), and aunt and uncles

With granddaughters Baylee and Rilee Hasselmann

The Endless Flight

This is a story about my adventure flying to Connecticut to see my newest grandchild, Jennifer, on August 16, 1996.

The story begins in Cincinnati, where I had completed a wonderful visit with my daughter Judy, her husband Don, and their boys, Bill, Jim, and Michael. I flew out of Cincinnati at 8:40 a.m. on a Northwest flight bound for Detroit, arriving at 10 a.m. My connecting flight, scheduled to depart at 10:35 and arrive at LaGuardia at 12:12, was delayed because of engine trouble.

At 12:20 p.m. (8 minutes after my scheduled arrival time in New York) we were informed that the flight was now canceled. The ticket agent told me that a flight would be leaving for New York in 20 minutes from the C concourse. With no baggage, I ran the mile between concourses only to find a long line in front of the ticket counter. I was eventually placed 68th on the standby list. The canceled flight had been on a jumbo jet; this flight, on a DC9, was not going to fit 68 extra passengers.

At another counter I inquired about future flights to New York, and was told I could take a flight to Minneapolis and connect with a flight arriving in New York around 9 that evening. It seemed a waste of a day arriving that late to see a baby, and as I poured out my tale of grandfatherly woe to the agent, another agent overheard my plea and took pity on me. She found a Northwest flight to Baltimore, leaving in half an hour, that would connect with a USAir flight scheduled to arrive at LaGuardia at 4:52 p.m. She cautioned that I would have only 15 minutes to change planes in Baltimore, but since the gates were adjacent, I should be able to make the connection.

Settling comfortably into my seat on the plane and feeling good that I was now on my way, I suddenly realized that we were not moving away from the gate on time; in fact, we were exactly 15 minutes late leaving. The cabin steward assured me that we would make up the time in flight. However, a half hour later, the captain announced that due to a storm ahead, we would have to circle for about 20 minutes. As we pulled into the gate in Baltimore I looked out the right side of the fuselage and saw a USAir plane being pushed away from its gate. The terminal monitor confirmed that it was indeed my flight that had just left. An agent promised to book me on the next USAir flight for New York, leaving at 7:30 p.m., or she could give me a voucher to take a taxi into Washington, D.C. There I could catch a 6 p.m. Delta shuttle to LaGuardia.

I chose the taxi option, and once again settled back in the seat thinking that I was at least getting closer to my destination. As we approached Washington the traffic thickened, then crawled, and finally stopped. Meanwhile, the promised storm arrived with a vengeance, accompanied by a spectacular lightning and thunder show.

Arriving at the Washington airport, I went immediately to the Delta shuttle counter and was told that all flights were grounded because of the storm. The shuttles might resume flying in two hours, or they might not. The last flight was scheduled to leave at 9 p.m.; I was given a red sticker with the number 41 and told to check back in an hour for an update.

This meant that when the storm lifted and service to New York resumed, I would board 41st on the next shuttle. Realizing that I might be stuck in Washington all night, I inquired at the Northwest counter about hotel and meal vouchers or free flights to make up for this miserable journey. The agent offered to put me on a 6:30 p.m. Northwest flight to New York as soon as it landed; it was circling because of the storm. I agreed, and he changed my ticket yet again and gave me a voucher for $5, which in those days nearly covered the cost of a slice of pizza and a beer.

I went to gate 3, as instructed, and saw the posting for a flight to Grand Rapids and Minneapolis. The agent looked at my ticket and said the gate for Detroit had been moved to gate 4.

With grandson Michael Loftus

"Detroit!" I yelled, "I don't want to go to Detroit! I left there 11 hours ago! I want to go to New York!" He looked at my boarding pass, which said "Detroit." He looked at me as if I were some kind of fruitcake, and asked, "Well, why didn't you take the shuttle?"

Speechless, I fled down the concourse and back to the Delta shuttle. I was relieved to see that the sun was now appearing from behind the clouds. I arrived at the gate as an announcement called for people with stickers 26–50 to board. I walked up, handed the agent my card, and boarded the plane.

Yet again, I settled back in my seat. It was now after 7 p.m. The engines were started, we began to taxi, and I felt relieved that I was on the final leg of this sojourn. However, as we taxied out near the end of the runway, the captain announced that another storm was blanketing the state of New York, and we

With granddaughter Jen Ongley

would have to wait a bit longer. We pulled over to a waiting area and sat, while the captain tried to comfort us by telling us that the plane parked next to us would take off just before us—when that plane took off, we would be next. We waited and waited. It became 9:30 p.m., and I knew that Washington had a

10 p.m. curfew. If we didn't leave in the next half hour, we were stuck for the night.

At 10 the plane next to us lit up and taxied away. I was sure it was headed back to the terminal, and we would follow. However, we taxied to the runway and at 10:10 p.m. took off, arriving in New York sometime after 11:30 p.m.

A person can drive from Cincinnati to New York in about 10 hours. My journey by air took 15. At LaGuardia I had to search the baggage area for my luggage and convince a sleepy guard to unlock the door to retrieve it. I secured a seat on the last limousine leaving for Connecticut and was met at the bus terminal by my son-in-law Steve. I was happy to greet my daughter Laurie at about 1 a.m., but had to wait until morning to see Jennifer.

With grandchildren Keegan Hasselmann (now Keegan Korthauer) and Dorian Hasselmann

However, once I saw baby Jennifer, my endless flight receded into the background. I would do it all again to see her!

With grandson Tyler Hasselmann

With grandsons Bill and James Loftus, my sweatshirt celebrating the former name of the Minnesota Orchestra

What's in a Name?

In 1968, twenty years after I joined the Minneapolis Symphony, the ensemble's name was changed to Minnesota Orchestra. There was a great deal of controversy caused by this change, especially among the musicians and public who liked their "hometown" association with the name Minneapolis. Orchestra members felt betrayed, believing that the great reputation built over 65 years of touring and recordings had been compromised.

Lack of name recognition was evident in 1972–1973 when, to celebrate the orchestra's 70th anniversary, we journeyed to Mexico to play in Mexico City's Bellas Artes hall. We played four concerts to very disappointing audiences. The first concert was played to 300 or 400 people, most of whom had traveled from Minneapolis. Nearly every Mexican music critic was reported to have written something like, "If only the music lovers of Mexico City had known that it was the famous Minneapolis Symphony Orchestra performing last night at Bellas Artes, they would have flocked to hear them."

On another occasion the orchestra played a concert in Sarasota, Florida, to an equally dismal audience. We saw posters around town announcing a concert by the University of Minnesota Orchestra at the same time and place as ours.

The ambiguity was corrected in subsequent programs and posters, where the name Minnesota Orchestra was followed by a tag, "Founded in 1903 as the Minneapolis Symphony." For two decades, I had to use both names when I told people where I was employed. Only in recent years, after many critically acclaimed recordings and tours, has the Minnesota Orchestra's reputation become secure under its new name.

Practicing golf in the backyard with Sparky, who caught the balls off the club

The concert in Terrace Mill, Minnesota

1812 Overture: What Could Possibly Go Wrong?

Tchaikovsky's *1812 Overture* is one of the most frequently performed pieces in the orchestral literature, especially during the summer months when orchestras play outdoor concerts. These concerts often end with spectacular displays of fireworks, overlapping with the cannon shots that conclude the overture. I have played the *1812 Overture* many times over many years, and I have witnessed an abundance of mishaps that accompanied the spectacular finishes.

Early in my career in Minnesota, the orchestra played on a modular portable stage in Rev. Martin Luther King Jr. Park. The stage where the percussion was set was so crowded that the three big chimes were placed sideways next to the trumpet section. As we approached the part of the overture that depicts the victory of the Russian army over the French, I noticed the hands of the percussionist who would ring the triumphant chime tones. He was clutching the mallets so tightly that his knuckles were white. His jaw was set tightly, and his eyes had a determined look. When the big moment came, the conductor gave him a tremendous cue, he hit the chimes with all his might, and one of the straps holding a chime snapped. The chime fell to the floor with an audible thunk. He continued to slam the other two chimes, and broke a second strap. That chime also thunked to the floor. He was left with only one chime, which he tapped with a mild "ding, ding, ding."

We played the *1812 Overture* once in the Metrodome, then the home of the Minnesota Twins. The inflatable dome over the stadium precluded fireworks during the music, so the audience was supposed to go outside for the pyrotechnics after the concert. Somehow the communication by walkie-talkie was garbled, and the fireworks began to boom well before the finale. People started leaving their seats to go outside and watch, leaving the orchestra to finish the overture with half an audience listening inside.

Powderhorn Park in South Minneapolis hosted an outdoor concert one July, not long after a young boy had been shot and killed nearby. Before the point in the Tchaikovsky when the battle scene begins, our two stagehands went into the orchestra truck to collect their rifles, which were used to simulate the cannons. Two policemen drew their pistols and demanded that the stagehands drop their weapons. By the time they could explain the reason for the rifles, the overture had ended. The finale finished rather meekly that year.

I only played once in Terrace Mill, Minnesota, but it is a concert I remember well. The outdoor setting was rustic, with the stage placed in front a huge barn-like structure next to a large pond. A herd of cattle grazed lazily beyond the pond, creating a pastoral atmosphere. Audience members sat on blankets or bales of straw. A dozen miniature cannons had been placed along the edge of the pond, to be fired in synchronization with the end of the overture. The concert went

Backstage with Larry Zalkind from the Sousa Band

smoothly until the cannons were fired. The noise so panicked the cattle that they stampeded over the hill out of sight, not to be seen the rest of the night.

One performance of the *1812 Overture* caused us to fear physical harm. At a concert overlooking the Mississippi River, the fireworks were so close to the orchestra that the burning ash and wrappers from the aerial bombs fell onto the orchestra. In our hurry to get out of the way, as soon as we finished playing we grabbed our instruments and cases and packed them up quickly. It wasn't until the next day that we discovered that some of the burning pieces had fallen into the bassoon trunk, had smoldered all night, and had destroyed the instrument and its case.

Audiences love the *1812 Overture,* and orchestras will no doubt continue to play it. But the combination of crowds, small stages, guns, and fireworks will just as likely continue to have comical (and occasionally disastrous) results.

With the Minnesota Orchestra trumpet section on the St. Croix River: (L to R) Doug Carlson, Manny Laureano, Bob Dorer, Chuck Lazarus

Not All Venues Are Suitable for an Orchestra

Venues for concerts are not always selected for reasons of acoustics or audience comfort. I remember one concert we played in the parking lot of a Lund's grocery store, with Mr. Lund listening from the roof of the store.

We wanted to play a concert on the Nicollet Mall, a pedestrian zone in downtown Minneapolis. We set up in front of Dayton's department store. The audience was separated from the orchestra by the mall, which was only problematic when city buses occasionally drove between the two groups.

Obstacles sometimes had to be creatively overcome. At an outdoor performance in Ladysmith, Wisconsin, the sun shone straight into the eyes of the string players. The glare made the music unreadable, and the players were concerned about the health of their instruments in the hot sun. The management, ever willing to solve problems, asked our truck driver to take the instrument truck up a hill and park it between the sun and the stage. With that artificial eclipse, the concert proceeded on schedule.

At another outdoor concert, in Hudson, Wisconsin, rain appeared imminent. To protect the stringed instruments, we switched places on stage: the string players sat in the back under the shell, and we brass players sat in front. In the end we all stayed dry, but we were ready.

At a concert in Plymouth, Minnesota, a hot-air balloon circled noisily above the audience. It landed right behind the audience, making concentration on the concert impossible.

In Sugar Hill, in northern Minnesota, a stagehand helpfully tuned up his car right next to the stage, during the concert.

The pavilion at Harriet Island, in Saint Paul, is a fine place for a concert. We were most impressed when Adam Kuenzel (principal flute) arrived for the concert by kayak.

Even Carnegie Hall provided adventures. Before one of our concerts began, a fire broke out in the hall. As the bass players were trying to wrestle their instruments down the stairs, they collided with firemen rushing with their hoses up the same stairs.

We encountered fire at the Carnegie Deli too. We were eating in an enclosed outdoor area, admiring the snow falling around us. Burning debris started falling from above, and Ron Balasz (violin) noticed that it was landing on the glass roof over our heads. He went to the maitre d' and said it was an emergency: there was a fire upstairs. The maitre d' said "If you don't like it, just get out." We took his advice, and as we left we heard fire trucks thumping through the deep snow toward the restaurant.

With Allan Dean and Jens Lindemann at the Midwest Bandmasters conference in 2019

Playing a solo with the Minnesota Orchestra in 1982, Keith Brion on the podium

An Unfortunate Conductor

Many years ago, a violinist in the Minneapolis Symphony named Pete Lisowsky decided to give up the violin and become a conductor. Pete had played under many famous conductors and watched how they performed and how they lived their lives, so he tried to pattern his life after theirs. He was aware how they took ships from Europe to conduct American orchestras, and how they traveled by train to guest conduct in various cities.

When he had a conducting engagement in Minneapolis, Pete would take the train from his home in St. Paul, check into a hotel, rest, then go to the rehearsal. After the rehearsal he would go back to his hotel, rest, have dinner, and take a taxi to the concert. After the performance he would return to the hotel, sleep overnight, and take the train home to St. Paul in the morning, just like the big-name conductors would do.

Pete was a kind and gentle man, but his conducting left a great deal to be desired. Every concert that I played under him had an unfortunate episode that bordered on disaster. During one concert when he was conducting "The Star-Spangled Banner," the tempo got so slow that it actually ground to a halt.

He appeared to be in a daze, then snapped out of it and hurried to the end of the anthem.

Another time when Pete was conducting "The Star-Spangled Banner," he gave a tremendous upbeat with both hands swinging toward each other. He stabbed his left hand with the baton in his right so hard that blood dripped down his white sleeve and coat.

At one concert, during Offenbach's *Orpheus in the Underworld,* he kept glancing down at the first violinist who was playing an important and exposed solo. Right in the middle of the solo, Pete looked down once more and said loudly, "You call that a solo tone?" The poor violinist got so flustered that he tightened up, and the playing got worse.

I was an accidental bystander to a performance at Central High School in St. Paul. The brass section was not needed for a four-movement symphony, so we left the stage and went into the hall. After playing the first two movements, Pete looked at his watch and decided that there was not enough time to finish the symphony. He signaled the orchestra to cut the last two movements and go immediately into the finale, selections from *My Fair Lady*. We watched helplessly from the audience as the orchestra played the finale without any brass.

A *Nutcracker* rehearsal at Northrop Auditorium, Minneapolis

For Lack of a Piano Chair

During the 1950s and 1960s, Ava Knardahl was the Minneapolis Symphony's pianist. A wonderful musician with a cheerful, warm personality, Ava found it more comfortable to play piano from a straight-backed chair than from a standard piano bench. Whenever she finished playing an especially difficult or fast passage, she would throw her hands into the air and lunge backward into the back of the chair. We all became accustomed to Ava's signature motion, and the stage crew knew to furnish her with the appropriate chair.

One day on tour, the stagehands were unable to locate a straight-backed chair for Ava, and set out a piano bench instead. The concert proceeded uneventfully until the moment when Ava finished a huge solo passage, whereupon she characteristically threw out her hands, lunged backward, and fell completely off the bench, crashing to the floor. Luckily, she was uninjured, except for the insult to her pride. Ever the professional, she crawled back up onto the bench and played her next passage on time.

With family members at Como Park in St. Paul

Teach Your Children Well

When my children were young, I always answered their questions with all the knowledge I had gained throughout my life. When they stumped me for a correct answer, I would make one up, hoping to carry on the myth that I was indeed the smartest person they knew. As the kids grew older, some of my answers caused raised eyebrows and doubtful responses such as, "Are you sure?" or "That doesn't seem possible!" I would counter with, "I'll always give you an answer, but it's up to you to ascertain whether it's a correct one or not." The kids started calling this Dad's Guaranteed Answer.

The Guaranteed Answer went on for many years with my profession as a symphony musician as my children grew into adulthood. My older daughter, Laurie, earned her doctorate in musicology from Yale. One day I had a burning question concerning some obscure musical term, so I called her for an expert definition. She gave me an answer that seemed plausible, yet not quite sound. "Is that right?" I asked. You guessed it—she said "I gave you an answer. It's up to you to decide whether it's a correct answer."

When my son David was three or four years old, he liked to sit on my lap when we were driving on an extended vacation and pretend he was driving the car. Naturally his hands would oversteer the wheel, but under his tender small body I had my fingers on the bottom of the steering wheel, holding the car steady.

Fast forward to when David was fifteen years old. He had been taking all the coursework and instruction to fly an airplane. On his sixteenth birthday I took him for his driver's license exam, which he easily passed. He dropped me off at home and took the car, alone, to the airport for his first solo flight. After more exams and training, he was soon ready to take a passenger on a flight.

We flew together from St. Paul to Rochester, Minnesota, following behind a 727 as we approached for a landing. The landing strip looked like a postage stamp, and I suddenly panicked. I don't know anything about flying, and here my sixteen-year-old son was about to attempt this unbelievable feat. Needless to say, he set the plane down perfectly, and my panic subsided into great admiration for his skills.

On the return trip, he asked me if I wanted to take the controls, to get the feel of flying. I was glad for the opportunity, and he instructed me to watch the nose of the plane and keep it level with the horizon. I tried with all my might to prove to him that "Dads can do everything," but I was aware of the nose dipping down every so often. However, I did not have to worry, as I could feel his

Four generations of Hasselmanns: With son David, grandson Dillon, and great-grandson Tristan

carefully concealed but confident fingers making the correction.

With Bea in 2009

Bea and Me

The first time I laid eyes on Bea Speed was at Orchestra Hall, when her Metropolitan Boys Choir was rehearsing with the Minnesota Orchestra for a performance of Mahler's Symphony No. 8 with Klaus Tennstedt. I was impressed with how professionally she handled the boys and how well they sang. I had the opportunity to talk with her backstage, and I found her to be personable and someone I would like to know better. After the concert that evening I sought her out, only to find her accompanied by a tall gentleman who I assumed was her husband or boyfriend. I filed her name and my feelings for her away in my memory for future investigation.

A few months later I was invited to play for a performance of Berlioz's Te Deum at a church in Apple Valley. This work requires a large orchestra and chorus, plus a boys' choir and several soloists. Standing in front of the boys' choir off to the side of the main conductor stood Bea, calmly and accurately conducting the boys' choir as she watched every nuance of the principal conductor's baton. As the rehearsal continued, I began to follow Bea,

Bea relaxing on the deck

because her beat was clearer than that of the staff conductor. I found out later that half the orchestra was also following her rather than the main conductor. I asked her if she would mind conducting all the time instead of only when the boys were singing. She declined, saying it would look silly for her to be conducting boys who were sitting still and not singing.

The more I watched, the more I was attracted to her, so at break I chatted with her about the choir and her teaching at Central High School. She asked me how I was going to spend the afternoon between the rehearsal and that night's concert; I told her that I was going home to bake chocolate chip cookies to send to my daughter Judy, away at college. Bea seemed impressed with that idea, and we went back to work.

Henry Charles Smith, associate conductor of the Minnesota Orchestra and former principal trombone in Philadelphia, was playing trombone in the Berlioz. I asked him if he knew Bea—he did, and recommended her warmly. Henry let me know that Bea was divorced, so I resolved to pursue my earlier interest. The next night I sought her out again, and she asked if I had brought any cookies for her to sample. I apologized that I hadn't, and then had the pleasure of watching her during another performance. Much

The matchmaker, Henry Charles Smith

My wedding to Bea, with my mother Evelyn

later I discovered that Bea had also called Henry, for a reference about me. Our relationship might never have gotten off the ground if Henry hadn't recommended both of us to each other.

I called Bea several times for a date before we found a night that she was free. The night before our date, I boxed up a small package of chocolate chip cookies and left them on her doorstep with a note saying that I was looking forward to our date, signed "Fondly, Ron." We went to see Benjamin Britten's opera *Billy Budd* at Northrop Auditorium. I'm sure the performance was a good one, but I honestly can't remember a thing about it. I was much too busy getting to know Bea.

We went out again later that week, driving to Rochester for a Minnesota Orchestra concert and stopping for dinner in Mantorville. As we entered the restaurant we saw many teenage couples in formal dress, eating dinner before the high school's senior prom. Bea commented that she was the only woman in the restaurant not wearing a corsage. After dinner, on the way out of the restaurant, I took a beautiful red rose from a vase on the table and gave it to Bea in the car. I was proud of my thievery, thinking that the restaurant staff would discard the flowers at the end of the evening anyway. Bea gently informed me that the flower was silk.

After many more dates, I asked Bea to marry me, and to my great happiness, she said "Yes." That was more than thirty years ago, and I am still in love with Bea Speed Hasselmann.

With Bea at a backyard picnic

With grandsons Bill and Michael Loftus after a successful skydiving adventure

Do We Want to Board That Plane?

On one of the Minneapolis Symphony tours of Eastern states during the 1960s, our tour manager, Glenn Cooke, arranged for the orchestra to be picked up by airplane at a small airport whose runway was surrounded by mountains. The orchestra arrived at the airport before our plane landed, so we all either rested in the tiny waiting room or wandered along the fence lining the runway. A small group of people also stood along the fence, searching the sky as if waiting for an arrival by air. I chatted with a local man about the area, the weather, and other pleasantries, then I asked him if he was waiting for someone to arrive on a flight. His answer astounded me: "No, I understand there is a four-engine plane coming in this morning. The last time a four-engine plane took off from this airport, three years ago, it crashed into that mountain at the end of the runway, and this time I don't want to miss it!" I mentioned this conversation to a number of colleagues, so when our DC-4 cleared the mountain at the end of the runway, we cheered that the poor fellow on the ground had been cheated. We were happy that he had wasted his morning coming out to the airport.

On a Texas Airways DC-3 we were assisted by a brand-new stewardess, who forgot to put the pin in the airplane's door. When the pilots revved the engine, the door fell outward. Once airborne, the stewardess did not tolerate turbulence well and got airsick. By the time we landed, her makeup was streaked and she was a mess.

Once we were taking off in a DC-3 next to a golf course. The pilot came on the intercom, "We have a slight delay. Some guy hit a ball onto the runway, and came in a golf cart to retrieve it." Can you imagine any of these incidents occurring today?

I flew safely out of Nacogdoches, Texas, although our personnel manager nearly made me miss the flight. We were to take two buses from the hotel and two Convair planes, each at slightly different times. I overslept and missed the first bus to the airport. I barely made it to the second bus. Manager Boris Sokoloff didn't want to let me ride the second bus, as there were no empty seats. Glenn Cooke fortunately noticed my absence at the airport and arranged for a seat on the second plane. I eventually prevailed and convinced Boris that I had to get on the second bus, so as to avoid being left in Texas. When we got to the airport, I was now on the second flight.

Celebrating my 80th birthday by jumping out of an airplane

In later years, our air travel was much more comfortable. Large airliners were quiet and smooth in comparison to the old DC-3s. On one flight from Minneapolis to Detroit I fell asleep as our plane taxied for takeoff, and I woke up as we were approaching the arrival gate. I thought we had taxied all the way from Minneapolis to Detroit.

Some orchestra members refused to fly, giving up their days off to take ground transportation. We called them the "ground crew." Ken and Nancy Rosen were a married couple in the orchestra, and when we flew in two planes, they made a point to fly separately, in case one of them crashed. When we started taking one plane rather than two, they lost that option.

One airline mishap was my own fault. When the orchestra toured in

Florida, there was nothing I liked better than fresh shrimp. I thought I was so clever, buying fresh shrimp, freezing it in a block of ice in a half-gallon milk carton, and packing it in my golf bag. I'd arrive home with cold shrimp. What could go wrong? That's right: I missed a connection in Atlanta, and the golf bag went to the lost luggage office. By the time I retrieved it in Minneapolis, the shrimp were a soggy, stinky mess. The ice had melted and disappeared—who knows how many other people's luggage were wet and smelly that day?

Playing ball with four-footed family members Lady and Prince

The man behind the horn

How Did We Survive All Those Car Trips?

In the days before so many safety features were added to automobiles, it's a wonder that I wasn't killed on the highways. Early one morning in 1953 I was riding in the middle of the back seat with Jimmy Featherstone's band, on our way to Arnolds Park in Indiana. Screeching tires woke me from a doze. Our car had been following a truck with brake lights caked in mud, and the truck stopped suddenly when the driver realized he wouldn't safely pass under a bridge. I found out later that our drummer, who was driving, had a glass eye and thus no depth perception. We hit the side of the truck, ripping off the fender and two doors of our car. We limped back to Chicago the next day with the doors tied on by rope.

After a Minnesota Orchestra concert in Mississippi, six of us got into a rented car so we could stay in the same town and play golf the next day, a free day. The orchestra bus left for the next town while we drove toward the hotel. John Sambuco (violin) wouldn't start the car until the rest of us fastened our seat belts; he saved our lives that night. Driving 70 miles per hour in the dark on a two-lane highway, John couldn't see anything but the oncoming headlights. A truck down in the ditch also shone its headlights toward us. A lumber truck preparing to turn left ahead of us was stopped in the road, with no tail lights. We slammed into that truck at 60 mph, no skid marks on the road. I had been sitting in the middle of the back seat, and after the crash I found my eyeglasses under the accelerator pedal. At the hotel I combed glass out of my hair; the following day I had a black and blue belt across my abdomen. George Stahl (bass), who was sitting in the front seat, got smacked on the back of the head by the one golf bag that hadn't fit in the trunk and was perched on the back ledge. We couldn't understand why George was complaining of knee pain the next day until we looked at the car in daylight and found the impressions of his knees in the dash.

Fanfare in the lobby of Orchestra Hall: Mike Hipps, me, Clem Volpe, Manny Laureano

With conductor Edo de Waart and concertmaster Jorja Fleezanis in 2012

No Respect for the Strings

Edo de Waart was giving beating instructions for Joan Tower's *Fanfare for the Uncommon Woman (#3)* to a double brass quintet in rehearsal: "Everyone get that?" We all nodded. "Oh, that's right, there are no string players here, so I don't have to keep repeating it."

In the last 8 bars of Strauss's *Ein Heldenleben*, I had to play a low F. The lowest note on a trumpet is F-sharp. To play this F, I had to push my slide way out, basically to make the F-sharp a half-step flat. When Fritz Reiner recorded this piece, he gave this passage to the trombone! Edo told me to play it with authority. He said that if Strauss had wanted the passage to be that soft, he would have given it to the violas.

How many viola jokes have I told over the years? Too many to count. Just a few examples:

Why are violists and lawyers alike? Everyone is relieved when the case is closed.

How do you get a violist to play downbow spiccato? Write a whole note with "Solo" above it.

What's the difference between a violin and a viola? The viola burns longer.

What's the difference between a violin and a viola? There isn't any difference. The violin just looks smaller because the players' heads are so much bigger.

Did you hear about the violist who bragged that he could play 32nd notes? The rest of the orchestra didn't believe him, so he proved it by playing one.

How are a violist's fingers similar to lightning? They never strike the same place twice.

Did you hear about the violist who dreamed she was playing Handel's *Messiah*? She woke up and realized that she was playing Handel's *Messiah*.

How can you tell that a violist is playing out of tune? The bow is moving.

Didn't I just give you a dog bone?

Sousa Band cornets with Chinese hosts

Epiphany through a Sousa Band

Faith: An unquestioning belief in God that does not require proof or evidence. In Hebrews 1:1, faith is "being sure of what we hope for, and certain of what we do not see." I am a person of faith: I am a Christian and a child of God. I believe that God directs my life through the Holy Spirit and that Jesus is my Savior. Of many moments in my life when I felt God's presence, the most striking came in 2010 when I was on tour with "Keith Brion's New Sousa Band."

Around 1980, conductor Keith Brion concocted a plan to recreate John Philip Sousa's band of the early 1900s. Keith meticulously followed Sousa's formula for musical programming. The band's uniforms are exact replicas of those worn by Sousa's band in the 1920s: each navy blue coat has 35 yards of swirling black braid, a velvet collar, and a golden pin. Keith studied Sousa's conducting mannerisms and stage appearance, and now imitates them on the podium. I was fortunate to join "Keith Brion's New Sousa Band" in the spring of 2003, when the band was to perform at the Meredith Willson music festival in Mason City, Iowa. One of the cornet players had to drop out because of illness. Keith remembered hearing me play John Hartmann's *Facilita* as a solo in a

Minnesota Orchestra pops concert in 1992, and he invited me to join the Sousa band. Since that weekend, we have played all over the United States and, most memorably, a ten-day tour of China in 2010. On that tour we performed in Shanghai, Yinchuan, Chengdu, Kunming, and Beijing.

It was in Kunming that I experienced an epiphany that was to profoundly shape my spiritual life. It began on the third day of the tour, January 2, 2010. The band was treated to a tour of botanical gardens outside the city. On the way back to Kunming for a scheduled lunch at a local restaurant, we encountered a road closure three blocks from the restaurant. The bus driver let us out, indicating the direction we were to go and assuring us that the hotel was nearby.

As we walked along, I was enthralled by the architecture and the many open-air booths on both sides of the avenue.

With Allan Dean from the Sousa Band

At lunch, I indicated to my fellow musicians my desire to go back and take some pictures of the culture we passed through, but to my dismay, no one was interested. As our hotel was supposedly nearby, they all opted to rest before the rehearsal that afternoon. Undaunted, I set out on my own, back to the area we had passed through, snapping picture after picture, taking sheer delight in the experience. Down one street and up another, I saw wonder after wonder. I tasted the food, talked to vendors, said "ni hao," and got smiles from bewildered merchants. I wandered for about an hour, then looked at my watch and realized that the bus taking us to our rehearsal would be leaving the hotel in 45 minutes. I tried to retrace my steps to the restaurant where we had lunch, remembering that the hotel was nearby. However, nothing looked familiar. I started vectoring, going in bigger circles, but only got more lost. Nervous and panicking, I realized that I could not remember the name of the hotel or the name of the concert hall. I had been given a card with the name of our hotel, but I had left the card in the pants pocket of my tuxedo, back at the hotel. I was lost in a city of 3 million people.

Even if I could find someone who spoke English, what could I ask them?

I looked at my watch again—the bus was scheduled to depart in fifteen minutes. I stopped in the middle of the sidewalk, looked up, and prayed: God, you are in control of my life. I am hopelessly lost! I don't know what to do! The band does not have a buddy system, or a check-off system to make sure everyone is accounted for. What can I do?

When I stopped, I had been walking next to a brick wall. I took eight or nine steps to a street corner and looked up to my right. There, about three blocks away, high at the top of a building in huge letters, was a sign in English, NEW ERA HOTEL. My hotel!! All our hotels on the tour were listed only in Chinese, but when we checked into this hotel in Kunming, we were greeted warmly with a sign in the lobby in English, "Welcome New Sousa Band to New Era Hotel."

I sprinted the three blocks to the hotel, raced up six flights of stairs, grabbed my uniform and cornet, dashed down to the lobby, bolted across the street to where the bus was already loaded, and sat down huffing and puffing. Three minutes later, we left.

My lifelong faith came to a pinnacle in those moments. Since the China trip, I have felt that this was my epiphany.

The banner that saved me from missing a concert in Kunming

Performing a solo with the Minnesota Orchestra in 1984

Mister Anonymous

Fame is fleeting, even for professional trumpeters. Several times in my career I had stars in my eyes after performing a solo, but for a variety of reasons I remained anonymous.

Shortly after I arrived in Minneapolis in 1958 I was hired by a group of Lutheran churches to play principal trumpet in a performance of Handel's *Messiah* in the old Auditorium. Of course, the performance included the bass aria "The Trumpet Shall Sound," which features a big trumpet solo. The performance went well, and I was pleased that my playing had all the beauty of sound and phrasing that I had intended.

The reviewer in the *Minneapolis Tribune* the next day was ecstatic about the performance. He wrote, "Handel's *Messiah* was brilliantly performed last evening in the Minneapolis Auditorium by the combined choirs from many area Lutheran churches with an orchestra of 75 members. The soloists were first rate and the conductor, Weston Noble, took tempos that brought out the beauty of each phrase. However, the high point of the performance was the trumpet solo in 'The trumpet shall sound.' It was as if Gabriel himself was blowing from heaven." He went on to identify the trumpet soloist as Ronald

Rasmussen. How he got Ronald Rasmussen from the program notes instead of Ronald Hasselmann, I never found out, but my greatest review of a performance left me anonymous.

With the Minnesota Orchestra I had a chance to be famous on a national broadcast. I was playing principal trumpet for a live broadcast of a concert that began with Beethoven's *Leonore Overture No. 3,* which has two exposed trumpet solos in the form of bugle calls. I was happy with my performance, and looked forward to listening to a tape of the broadcast when I got home that night. The broadcast announcer was complimentary about the solos, but ended with, "and now the conductor Stanislaw Skrowaczewski is motioning for

With Mitch Miller backstage in 1998

the trumpet soloist to come on stage for a bow, and here he comes, Merrimon Hipps Jr." My colleague Mike Hipps was a fine player, but these were not his solos.

Charles Schlueter, the orchestra's principal trumpet, took a leave of absence in the summer of 1976 to play in the Casals Festival Orchestra in Puerto Rico. In Charlie's absence, I became acting principal trumpet of the Minnesota Orchestra.

1976 was the U.S. bicentennial year, and both Aaron Copland and Mitch Miller came to Minnesota to conduct American programs. Mitch Miller was well known at that time from his 1960s weekly television show, *Sing Along with Mitch.* While a television choir sang popular songs, the words of the songs appeared at the bottom of the screen to help the audience sing along. After the show was canceled, Mitch turned to guest conducting. In late June 1976 he performed an all-Gershwin program in Minnesota: *An American in Paris, Concerto in F for Piano and Orchestra,* and *Rhapsody in Blue,* all with prominent trumpet solos. These are works that regularly appear on trumpet audition lists.

In that month's *Showcase* magazine, Mary Ann Feldman, our program annotator, wrote, "Orchestra News of musicians' activities this summer: Lea Foli was off to the music festival in Gunnison, Colorado, and Charles Schlueter is playing in the Casals Festival Orchestra in Puerto Rico. In his absence, Clement Volpe is playing principal trumpet." I confronted Mary Ann one day in the hallway of Orchestra Hall and asked her how she could write that Clem was playing first trumpet. She said, "I just took the next name in line from the orchestra roster." I showed her the roster in the program, where Charles Schlueter was listed as principal, then I was listed as associate principal, then Clem's name was listed under mine. I have no idea how she skipped my name to pick up Clem's.

Two weeks later, for the July Bicentennial celebration, Aaron Copland conducted a nationally televised program that included Charles Ives's *Decoration Day*. This piece depicts a New Orleans–style funeral, beginning with a solemn procession to the cemetery, pausing for the playing of "Taps," and concluding with a jazzy, swinging, Dixieland-style recessional. Before the televised performance, I couldn't help but think of the bugler who played "Taps" at Kennedy's funeral in 1963 and the look of sheer terror in his eyes while he waited to play. He did muff a few notes, but I'm sure there was not a trumpet player in the world who would have wanted to trade places with him at that time. I almost succeeded in shutting out that image, but when I looked up at Copland on the podium, I could see the television camera in the first tier over his left shoulder, with two red lights indicating that the camera was live and recording. In the stage light reflection, I could also see the lens revolving, telling me that the camera was bringing me into close focus. I was, after all, the only one playing. Somehow I played "Taps" perfectly, but I felt my heart pounding for several minutes afterward. My reputation remained intact regionally after the live broadcast, but the national broadcast was delayed, and in order to fit the program into 90 minutes, the producers cut *Decoration Day*. Fame is so fleeting!

Even celebrities such as Mitch Miller suffered occasional anonymity. After his first rehearsal in Minnesota in 1976, he invited me to lunch at a local restaurant. We sat down and he began to regale me with stories about his life as a big-time star. He began talking rather loudly about conducting the New York Philharmonic and other orchestras as the waitress stood patiently waiting to take our order. I innocently asked her, "Do you know who this gentleman is?" She replied, "I don't have a clue." Poor Mitch deflated like an old basketball. We spent the rest of the meal talking about our orchestra, realizing that this might be his last opportunity to end a Minnesota Orchestra concert with his trademark sing-along.

Playing a solo at a summer pops concert

Undeserved Fame

It's true that sometimes I was undeservedly anonymous. But it's also true that sometimes I got more applause than I deserved. The orchestra flew to Storm Lake, Iowa, for a concert with Eiji Oue conducting. Mike Hipps and I were scheduled to play only the encore, the *Hungarian March* by Berlioz, because the rest of the program took two trumpets. When we arrived in Storm Lake we collected our per diem and had dinner. We killed time while the orchestra played the first half of the concert. We suited up for the second half, a Beethoven symphony. At the conclusion of the Beethoven, during the applause, we slipped into our places. The applause continued, so Eiji gave solo bows. The first two trumpets got their solo bow, then he motioned for Mike and me to stand. We got acknowledged, the applause died, and we never played a note.

Once during the "rug concert" era of the 1970s, Leonard Slatkin was conducting a Baroque marathon. The second piece on the program called for one trumpet, me. To accommodate the marathon concert, the start time was moved to 7 p.m. rather than 8. I forgot about the earlier start time, so I arrived at the hall at my usual 7:10 p.m. Leonard announced the second piece and explained to the audience how orchestras in this period added trumpets. But when he turned around, there was no trumpet player! He rearranged the program on the fly, and performed the third piece instead. When I walked out for the second piece, now being played in the third spot, all eyes were on me! I didn't play until the final movement, which really confused the audience.

In Madison, Wisconsin, I was to play the backstage trumpet solo for Beethoven's *Leonore Overture No. 2*. Skrowaczewski showed me exactly where he wanted me to stand, way backstage by his dressing room, and I set my stand and music there. We had loaned these parts to another orchestra, and someone who couldn't transpose had written out the B-flat part in concert pitch on the part. I had to run down the hall to hear my cue, and back again to play my solo. In my hurry I got confounded by the multiple staves on the page, so I played horribly. I moved the set-up closer for the second call, and I ignored the score and played from memory. This second solo went fine. After the performance I was relieved to find out that nobody could hear a note of the first call.

At a reception with (L to R) Ross Tolbert, Myrna Rian, Leonard Slatkin, and Angela Fuller.

Backstage with Minnie Mouse in 1987

What's in a Name: Redux

Before the 1970s, the Minnesota Orchestra played many concerts in small towns around the state of Minnesota. Many of the small-town stages were too small to accommodate all the players, or the towns could not afford the cost of the entire orchestra, so we often divided into two smaller orchestras. Half the orchestra would play in one town while the other half played in another town. (The St. Paul Chamber Orchestra, an excellent but smaller ensemble, later served this regional touring function.)

Because both halves of the symphony were called "Minnesota Orchestra," the organizers devised a system of referring to one group as "Orchestra X" and the other "Orchestra Y." It was common for musicians to ask each other, "Which orchestra are you in?" The reply would be either "Orchestra X" or "Orchestra Y."

One night my half of the orchestra was assigned to bus to Winona for a concert, and we stopped for dinner beforehand at the Hot Fish House. Because it was winter, most of the musicians brought their instruments into the restaurant to keep them warm. As we filed past a table with two women eating dinner, one of them asked Elliot Fine (percussion), "What orchestra is this?" Inevitably, he replied with all seriousness, "Orchestra X."

With DJ Barraclough and Brian Neal from the Dallas Brass, and local musician and good friend Bill Webb

Backstage with Maurice André

Auditions Don't Always Go As Planned

I was fortunate in my audition history; most prospective orchestra members are not so lucky. It is common for 200 applications to be received for a single opening, which means that 99.5% of the applicants will be unsuccessful. During my tenure as personnel manager of the Minnesota Orchestra I had occasion to talk to many candidates who performed less well than they had anticipated at their auditions. A few candidates in particular stick in my memory.

In 1995 I asked one player how his audition had gone. He replied, "I drove 1,500 miles to come here and play like shit."

A couple of years later I asked a double bass candidate the same question. He lamented, "Oh, man, I was so prepared for this audition. I had the excerpts down cold—my solo was gorgeous. I played for friends who told me there was no way I could lose the audition if I played like that. I've been practicing yoga. I was pumped. Even when you opened the door for me to walk on stage, I felt confident. But when you said to the committee, 'This is candidate number 127,' I lost it. I thought, 'What could I possibly do better than the 126 candidates who went before me?' and I immediately crashed and burned. My hands started shaking and my playing fell apart. My vibrato was uneven; my tone was forced; and my technique was one big jumble of mush." All I could do for this poor fellow was thank him for coming and extend best wishes for future auditions.

We received a resume from Miss Coeur d'Alene, Idaho. Her resume read "Concertmaster of Coeur d'Alene Orchestra" and "Coeur d'Alene" this and that. She was very pleasant to talk to as she prepared for her violin audition. I went into her warm-up room to explain about the liveliness of the hall, the screen, and so on. I encouraged her to take her shoes off before walking on stage (so the committee wouldn't hear her heels clicking and be tipped off about her gender), to play a few notes before beginning her solo to hear the acoustic, to ask me any questions during the audition that I would then relay to the committee—the usual checklist of advice. I returned to the warm-up room about 10 minutes ahead of the audition to give her the exact list of excerpts that she would play. She said "I don't have that Mozart symphony." I offered to give her a copy of the excerpt and push her audition later, to give her a chance to practice it. She declined, "No, that's OK, I'll just play it." I heard later from a committee member that the violinist began the Mozart excerpt at a very slow tempo. The committee asked her to speed it up, and she kept plodding at a slow tempo. Unsurprisingly, she didn't get the job.

In my early years in the orchestra, one candidate took the bus all the way from Colorado to audition. In those days, air travel was dangerous in the winter, and he didn't want to chance it.

Ron Balazs (violin) and I were co–personnel managers for several years. At a trombone audition, a candidate tried to bribe me with $5,000. I told Ron about this, and he was justifiably upset: the candidate had offered Ron only $3,000.

A whistler sent in an audition tape to see if we would hire him as a soloist. Professionally he was a doctor, and to sweeten the pot he enclosed a scalpel. We didn't invite him for an audition.

I enjoyed watching a Japanese percussion candidate, who knelt and spread all his mallets on the floor in a fan shape before going in to the audition.

Some candidates had professional studios make their audition tapes. Others were more homegrown, such as the trombonist who sent in a tape with a dog barking in the background.

With daughter Laurie in the new Vikings stadium

Musicians Are Sports Fans Too

In the 1970s, the Minnesota Vikings were often in the playoffs. Orchestral musicians were football fans as much as anyone else, and in December we

hated Sunday afternoon *Nutcracker* matinees that conflicted with Vikings games. Frank Winsor (horn) figured that since he was deep in the orchestra pit, nobody would notice if he brought his tiny TV set with him to a matinee. He had been playing *Nutcracker* for many years, and had no worries about missing any entrances. But unknown to Frank, even

With Laurie at a Minnesota Twins game after I played the national anthem with Twin Cities Trumpet Ensemble

though the audience couldn't see his TV screen, they could see the glow of the screen against Frank's face. He was discovered, and management gave him holy hell after the show.

When the Twins played in the World Series in 1965, announcer Halsey Hall said during the radio show, "Well, folks, we appreciate your listening to our broadcast. Let us know where you are while you're listening to the play-by-play." I was tempted to call in and let Halsey know that our entire French horn section was playing a Young Audience concert with earplugs wired to a little radio.

Twin Cities Trumpet Ensemble in 2018

The one and only Steve Zellmer

Steve Zellmer

Steve Zellmer, trombonist, was a close friend and a quick-witted comedian. He was especially entertaining to have at dinners on tour. Frank Winsor (horn) and I would always follow Steve's recommendations for restaurants, knowing that he had diligently studied the possibilities.

At Emma's Bar in River Falls, Wisconsin, with Steve and Frank, we noticed a sign, "Champagne $5." Steve naturally said, "Let's have champagne!" He gave Emma $10 and was waiting for his change while we sipped. He finally said, "Hey, Emma, you said champagne was $5." She replied, "The set-up is $4.95." Steve fired back, "Hey, Emma. You owe us 5 cents."

In Rochester, Minnesota, a bunch of us entered a restaurant in black suits. The waitstaff asked us if we were businessmen. Zellmer replied, "No, we're Methodist ministers at a convention."

A similar punchline was delivered in Alexandria, Minnesota, though this time not by Zellmer. Twenty or so orchestra members were relaxing in the pool at a Holiday Inn. A waitress asked us if she could serve us anything. I suggested, "Anybody want a pink squirrel?" Unanimous replies of "Yes, me too."

The waitress returned with twenty cocktails, laughing. She said that when she placed the order, the bartender asked, "What have you got, a pool full of Sunday school teachers?"

Zellmer relayed that once he was walking his bulldog by Cedar Lake. A couple of boys walked by, and Steve heard them say, "That man looks just like his dog." Steve added, "That was the nicest compliment anyone ever gave me."

Steve visited St. Patrick's Cathedral in New York when the new Pope John Paul II was also visiting, shortly after his predecessor had died. When Steve returned, we asked "How was the Pope?" He replied, "He's much better. He is sitting up again."

Steve kept us entertained, but he did once cost me some expensive car repairs. Our brass quintet was on the road in my family's International Harvester Travelall. We stopped for gas in a small town, and the woman at the register noted our black suits and asked us what our business was. Steve told her we were federal investigators, suspicious of drugs in the local high school. She was aghast, and Steve stretched the story out, "We think they're smuggling the drugs into the cafeteria in the chili." I was embarrassed enough to hurry out of the station, not bothering to check the engine oil. Before I reached the end of that tank of gas, the oil ran out and the engine stopped working. I cringed as I paid the repair bill, thinking, "If I had only checked the oil in that town . . . ."

In New York our standard go-to (other than the Carnegie Deli) was Luchow's, a German restaurant. Frank and Steve and I were eating while listening to a piano trio play Viennese waltzes and similar light classics. The violinist must have been in his 70s or 80s. Musicians ourselves, we applauded enthusiastically after each number. During a break, the violinist came to thank us for our applause, and asked if we had any requests. Zellmer asked, "Do you know any Wagner?" The players were thrilled—they launched into the *Tannhäuser* overture and played their hearts out. We gave them a standing ovation when they finished, and the other patrons heard applause and stood up and applauded too. I could just picture the trio going home and telling their wives, "Brünnhilde, I got to play Wagner at Luchow's tonight."

Postscript: Some years later, after Zellmer had left the orchestra, we were on tour in Germany. A group of brass players was listening to a restaurant quartet of guitar, strings, and piano playing typical restaurant fare of polkas and the like. I was telling our trombone section the story of Luchow's, and they egged me on to repeat the scene. So I asked the players if they could play any classical music, like maybe some Wagner. They motioned to the server, "These guys want us to play Wagner." The server, clueless, asked, "Is that some sort of a song?" More proof that memorable experiences can rarely be repeated.

Dinner on tour with (L to R) Frank Winsor, Bernie Adelstein, and Les Davis

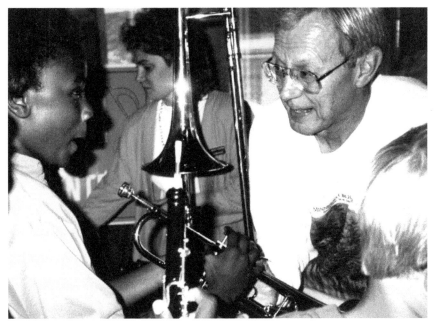

Encouraging young instrumentalists

Young Audience Concerts: Who Are the Kids?

The Minnesota Orchestra plays young people's concerts for large groups of children, and also sends chamber ensembles out into schools. My brass quintet played innumerable performances in gyms and auditoriums all over the upper Midwest. I had a routine about what makes a brass instrument, using a garden hose and a funnel to recreate tubing and a bell. I started this routine making mouthpieces out of wooden spools, but the result was never satisfactory. In my later years I used a regular trumpet mouthpiece and got a good approximation of a brass sound. The interaction between performer and audience was always interesting, and sometimes amusing.

Clem Volpe (trumpet) posed a question to the audience at a Catholic school, where all the kids wore uniforms with blue shirts. He called on "You, in the blue shirt." Ross Tolbert (tuba) asked a question of a group of students, and several raised their hands. Ross called on "You in the red shirt." The kid looked down to see if he was wearing a red shirt before he answered.

One of our players was introducing a piece by Johann Sebastian Bach, and asked, "Bach was famous for something that starts with the letter F—can anyone tell me what that was?" He expected someone to answer "fugue," but all we could think of was Bach's 20 children, and we had to stall for time before we could control our smirks enough to play again.

Being silly with my mother in 1999

Bugler's Holiday in 1996: Jeff Tyzik, Mike Hipps, me, Steve Wright, Doc Severinsen, and Allen Vizzutti, with Eiji Oue on the podium

Audiences Are Unpredictable

All of our performing would be a waste of time without our audiences. What did they think of our concerts? We typically received accolades, but a few attendees had different opinions.

On tour at a college gymnasium in DeKalb, Illinois, we played the long first movement of Mahler's Symphony No. 9. Skrowaczewski heard noises from the audience, so without turning around he asked concertmaster Lea Foli if people were coming into the hall. Lea looked out at the audience and replied, "No, they're leaving."

At Northrop Auditorium we played a piece by Henry Brant, in which players were placed around the interior of the hall. The newspaper review the next day complained, "Mr. Brant, your music was awful. In fact, it was so awful I tried to leave, but you fooled me: you had all the exits blocked with musicians."

At a concert at Grambling College, half the audience left partway through the performance, but they came back into the hall later. They had ducked out to watch a Cassius Clay fight.

After André Watts gave a glittering performance, an audience member who had sat in the front row had the opportunity to meet him. She told this world-class pianist, "You've got great ankles."

I played the solo part in Levy's "America" on tour in Canada, and discovered that we hadn't done our research. At one point the solo tune has "My Country 'Tis of Thee." The entire audience, hearing "God Save the Queen," stood up. The solo continues with variations on the melody, leaving the audience not knowing whether to stand or sit, so they did some of each.

On tour, a patron asked Laurie Green what instrument she played. Laurie said, "Second violin." The patron replied, "Oh, I'm so sorry."

On tour we often played in college gyms. Once we played the *Firebird Suite* to an audience sitting on folding chairs. In the front row, on the cello side, a young man sat between a young woman and an older woman, perhaps his date and his mother. When the orchestra finished the long quiet movement and hit the loud chord that begins the Infernal Dance, the young man jerked awake from a nap with both arms out to the side, hitting both women in the face. All three fell backward into the row of people behind them.

In 1995 the orchestra played Tomiko Kohjiba's *Hiroshima Requiem.* Many local citizens protested the playing of this piece, and staged candlelight vigils in Peavey Plaza. Police were on duty during the concert in case of any disturbance. Inside the hall Carl, the police sergeant in charge, had two officers standing in back. When the piece was over and the applause began, a woman started down the outer aisle in a fast walk toward the stage. The two cops began to bolt after her, but abruptly halted when they saw Eiji bow to her and she bow to him in return. The woman turned out to be the composer, whom Eiji had previously asked to come forward for a bow. Carl later said that if he had put two of his younger and dumber officers on duty instead of the older and wiser men, they would have tackled and handcuffed her before anyone could blink, right in front of the stage.

Antal Dorati

Antal Dorati

It seems only fitting that I devote a short chapter to the conductor who hired me into the Minnesota Orchestra, Antal Dorati. He had a way with words . . . .

On tour in the Dorati days, we always prepared two encores. At intermission the librarian went around backstage and told us which encore(s) Dorati had selected. In Edmonton, Alberta, we were expecting to play the Air from Bach's Orchestral Suite No. 3, then Berlioz's *Rákóczi March*. But we were rushing through the concert in order to catch a late train, and near the end of intermission Dorati decided to skip the Air. The librarian didn't manage to get word to everyone, so at the downbeat, half the orchestra started playing Bach and the other half started playing Berlioz. Dorati stopped conducting and said, "No, no, the other one." When we all switched pieces, half the orchestra was still playing each piece.

In a particularly difficult piece, I asked Dorati if he could throw me a helpful cue. Looking nervously at the score, he said, "I'm sorry, I can't give you a cue. I'm too busy conducting."

Preparing to play the "Promenade" solo in *Pictures at an Exhibition,* I asked Dorati how he was conducting it. He said, "It's simple. The first bar is in 5/4, so I conduct in a small circle. The second bar, in 6/4, is a bigger circle. You divide circle by 5 and then by 6."

Even when he beat a clear pattern, it wasn't always the correct one. He began conducting the overture to Mozart's *Marriage of Figaro,* one of the most well-known (and duple-time!) of all overtures, in a three pattern. He started "The Star-Spangled Banner," written in 3/4, in a four pattern. Whenever he got lost, he started conducting in big circles. Luckily, works such as these examples are well known by the players so the orchestra was able to continue on its own.

With conductors Eiji Oue and Stanislaw Skrowaczewski

Stanislaw Skrowaczewski

The comedian Danny Kaye performed often with symphony orchestras. Among other skits, he would conduct the orchestra in imitation of the regular conductor. After watching from the wings as Stanislaw Skrowaczewski conducted the overture to *Die Fledermaus,* Kaye remarked, "I can't caricature that man—he is his own caricature." As he walked out on stage he had a handful of batons, tossed them and tripped over them, and they went flying into the audience.

For one program Mike Hipps and I didn't play the Brahms Symphony No. 3, which calls for only two trumpets. Skrowaczewski started a morning rehearsal with Brahms, so Mike and I walked down the street for breakfast. We should have had plenty of time. But over breakfast we started worrying that if Skrowaczewski ran through the symphony without stopping, we would be late for the next piece, which required four trumpets. We ran back to the hall. As we entered the auditorium we heard the same opening 8 bars that were being rehearsed when we left.

In contrast, once Skrowaczewski started a rehearsal with Mendelssohn's Symphony No. 4, and he led us through the entire first movement without stopping. At the conclusion, he said, "This is terrible—there is nothing left to rehearse." We were happy to play an entire movement without stopping, and we were thrilled that he found no faults to correct. But he asked us to go back to the beginning anyway, and when our concentration relaxed, he found things that needed rehearsing.

Skrowaczewski had bad eyesight, so he sometimes asked players to read aloud the rehearsal numbers. At a rehearsal in Tempe, Arizona, Skrowaczewski said, "Give me a number." One of the oboe players retorted, "9-1-1."

At a recording session for Prokofiev's *Scythian Suite* in 1978, Mark Kelly (bassoon) complained that a passage was out of tune. Skrowaczewski answered, "That's the charm of this piece."

Skrowaczewski conducted the Symphony Ball, an annual fundraiser, and people were dancing. He started Ravel's *La Valse,* which begins in a lovely

Visiting the Kelly Copper Mine, Montana, in 1960.
I like to call this photo "Outstanding in his field"

waltz tempo. But the piece was intended for stage performance, not dancing, and its rhythm is irregular. People couldn't figure out whether to speed up, slow down, or sit down.

Mike Hipps and I were playing the Mozart Piano Concerto. No matter how softly we played, Skrowaczewski held up his hand as though he wanted less. I asked later, "Is that signal for the trumpets and timpani, or just me? Skrowaczewski answered, "I just want to be sure." From then on, Mike and I would always play louder than we thought he wanted, so we'd have room to decrease.

I was playing the trumpet solo in the Ives Symphony No. 2, and I couldn't figure out the rhythm. I went to Marv Dahlgren, percussionist and rhythm guru, for help. Marv couldn't count this rhythm either. So I figured I'd just play it, and Skrowaczewski would correct me if I got it wrong. I played the passage at the first rehearsal, and Skrowaczewski stopped. "First trumpet, Mr. Hasselmann . . . ." He tried to explain it, but he couldn't figure it out either. After some mumbling, he ended up saying, "Play it bravura!"

Marriner always placed his baton between his teeth when he needed to turn a page in rehearsal. Yo-Yo Ma poked fun at him by doing the same with his bow.

Neville Marriner

Unlike the other conductors regularly on the orchestra's podium, Neville Marriner spoke English natively. His turns of phrase were more clever than accidental.

At the first rehearsal after he became music director of the Minnesota Orchestra, Marriner opened with, "I was most touched by the enthusiasm you showed by my arrival at the airport yesterday. I only hope you won't be quite as enthusiastic at my departure."

After hearing a rough sound from the violins during rehearsal, Marriner remarked, "Sounds like someone has a new blade in their bow!"

Also too rough was a passage marked "Come il notturno." Marriner asked the orchestra, "Don't you know how to play 'Come il notturno'?" John Tartaglia (viola) piped up, "Not since I was a teenager."

Marriner sympathized with the difficulties of my adjunct job. He commented, "Being a personnel manager is like trying to dance in a nightclub. No matter what you do, you rub somebody the wrong way."

Talking to Phil Myers (horn) regarding a big crescendo, Marriner asked, "In your climb to glory, how legato can you make it?"

To the brass, to keep tempo from dragging, "You are the dominant figure here. However wrong you are, we shall believe you." He was also encouraging to the cello section, "You are our rhythmic conscience here." But he wasn't always complimentary: he once said that bass trombones have two dynamics, On and Off.

Marriner wasn't always specific in his verbal directions. He told us to "Crescendo to nowhere in particular. Make it an *f*." But he was always descriptive: "You might play the crescendo a bit louder, so when you decrescendo you won't end up with a hole in your pocket."

For a few years our viola section had a high rate of absenteeism. Before one concert I informed Marriner that the entire viola section was present, and he quipped, "What a good opportunity for a class photo."

I did enjoy Marriner's off-color jokes, but I won't repeat them here. Perhaps when we meet over a beer someday.

With Neville Marriner and WCCO radio legend Charlie Boone

Backstage with Erich Leinsdorf

Guest Conductors

I have played under more guest conductors than I can count. Most were competent, many were forgettable, and a few were so awful that I can't write about them publicly. A few particular moments remain vivid in my memory.

Erich Leinsdorf found creative ways to describe the sound he wanted. To a violinist playing the solo in *Der Rosenkavalier,* "Play lightly, as if you were a little drunk from too much champagne." To a string section, "If you can't play it, fake it, but fake it more convincingly." To a soloist who was playing timidly, "If you are naked, you look better if you smile." When rehearsing Haydn's "Surprise" Symphony, "This is real humor, not forced obscenities." When rehearsing a Mozart symphony, "Mozart school of puppeteering is not to my liking. I prefer it warm and lyrical." When describing articulation that should be neither too short nor too long, "Medium rare." To a violin soloist and an oboist who couldn't synchronize their rhythm, "Don't think it through intellectually. Once in a while use luck. As Napoleon said, 'Give me a general who has luck over one who works everything out in detail.' Now let's see if the luck holds up. Of course, if you solfege it, all right, that would also help."

Eri Klas, to achieve a pianissimo, "You should play as if you are carrying a candle slowly with a hand cupped around it so it does not blow out. You, on the other hand, are playing as if you are shining a flashlight back and forth."

Libor Pešek tried to be collaborative: "We are slowing down. What do you suggest?" The reply from the oboe section: "Conduct faster."

Aaron Copland asked for Schumann. Someone in the orchestra wanted to clarify, "Which one, William Schuman or Robert Schumann?" Copland's answer: "Bill not Bob."

Anton Horner, a horn player in the Philadelphia Orchestra, was trying to play softly enough for Leopold Stokowski. After trying to play the passage softer and softer, he rose, brandishing his horn, and said, "There are 16 feet of pipe in this, and if I don't blow in, nothing comes out."

Carmen Dragon conducted a rehearsal for a pops concert at Grant Park, Chicago, during the 1957–1958 season. Steve Zellmer (trombone) discovered that Dragon was conducting from a piano score rather than a full orchestral score. Halfway through the rehearsal, Steve closed his book and began playing the melody of each piece instead of his written trombone part. By the time of the concert, Dragon had become used to hearing the trombone playing the melody, and he began throwing cues to Steve for all the tunes.

Gianandrea Gavazzeni was a master of Italian opera and a stickler for rhythm. His refrain to the orchestra was "Vatcha the beat, vatcha the beat." But even he lost concentration once in a while. At a performance of the overture to Verdi's *La forza del destino,* he conducted the first big chords in the brass and then gestured to the cellos for the quiet tune. When the brass played the next big chords instead, he was so shocked that his glasses flew into the audience.

Edo de Waart gave us a visual image of the fifth movement of Berlioz's *Fantastic Symphony:* "You must sound like elves in tutus."

Rafael de Burgos liked to throw cues in Rimsky-Korsakov's *Capriccio Espagnol* as if he were a toreador prodding a bull. At one peformance our percussionist had been keeping his eye on the timpanist, who was feeling queasy, in case he had to take over the timpani part. When it came time for the tambourine solo, de Burgos threw a huge cue, which the percussionist watched while seated with his arms folded. He had gotten so wrapped up in the timpani part, he completely lost track of his own. When no tambourine sounded, a deflated de Burgos looked as though he had thrown a spear at a bull and missed.

Raymond Leppard philosophized in 1986, "I always go under the assumption that the composer knows best, unless otherwise proven wrong." And to the viola section, "We are quite exposed here, but not quite to the arrestable point." On musicality, "It's a better tune than you're making it."

Even the most collaborative conductor can be brought up short by an orchestra member. During a rehearsal our percussionist requested a cue from Philippe Entremont. When the time came and Entremont threw the cue, the percussionist pointed to himself and said, "Who, me?"

At a beer garden in England with the Mississippi River
Brass Band

Props

Orchestral percussionists sometimes need to employ nonstandard instruments, and the extra equipment doesn't always operate as planned. At the Lake Harriet bandshell, Floyd Thompson stood at a microphone in front of the orchestra to play Leroy Anderson's *Sandpaper Ballet*. He didn't put blocks under the sandpaper, and about halfway through the piece his hands were burning from the friction. The sound of sandpaper scratching was punctuated with Floyd's "Ow!" and "Ooh!"

Stanislaw Skrowaczewski was dissatisfied with the orchestra's biggest chime as he rehearsed Berlioz's *Fantastic Symphony*. He wanted bigger, deeper. For the second rehearsal the equipment manager brought in a bigger chime; it still wasn't big enough. The manager located an 8-foot chime at the University of Wisconsin, but he wouldn't be able to get it to the hall in time for any rehearsals. Skrowaczewski approved the import, even though he wouldn't hear the bell until the performance. Because the orchestra didn't own a stand big enough to hold the chime, on the afternoon of the concert it was suspended from the ceiling over the stage. At the performance, our part-time percussionist sat proudly next to this monster bell until time for the "Witches' Sabbath." He climbed the stepladder next to the suspended chime, raised his sledgehammer, and struck the chime. Bong! A glorious sound! Skrowaczewski beamed, and the audience felt the vibrations through their bodies. But there was a catch: the player needed to strike the chime again, and it had started swinging on its rope suspension. When it was time to sound another note, he swung at the chime, now out of his reach, and barely brushed the edge of the

With my mother Evelyn and a perfectly grilled Thanksgiving turkey

metal. Dink! At one point the poor player had to grab the top of the chime to keep from falling off the ladder. The brass section doubled over in laughter, unable to play for several measures.

When we took Respighi's *Pines of Rome* on tour, our percussionist used a phonograph recording to represent the birdcalls. He didn't test the phonograph player ahead of one concert in Canada, and during the performance it blew a fuse and cut power to the stage. The player attempted to spin the 45 record by hand. His revolutions were too slow, so it sounded like the pines were inhabited by a 90-pound canary. Naturally, those of us in the orchestra who could whistle started tweeting birdcalls. It was a classic fiasco.

In Rochester, Minnesota, our principal percussionist was playing tam-tam. He got engrossed in listening to the piece and lost his place. Paul Culp, another percussionist, realized that the principal was lost when he wasn't preparing to play a few bars before his tam-tam entrance. She warned him and started counting down the measures, "4-2-3-4, 3-2-3-4," and so on. The principal player recognized the timing, but in his hand he was holding only a little xylophone mallet, nowhere near heavy enough for the tam-tam. So he took off his shoe and whacked the gong with the heel.

Adventures with props weren't always in the percussion section. I was in the balcony of Orchestra Hall to play the solo part to Ives's *Unanswered Question*. The bulb on the stand light burned out, so I couldn't see my music. An usher helpfully held a cigarette lighter for me, and I was able to play the solo. I found out later that the flickering of the shadows from air currents on the flame created an eerie effect from the main floor.

Lake Wobegon® Brass Band in 2020

Strength in Community

When I retired after forty-two years as a member of the Minneapolis Symphony/Minnesota Orchestra, I found myself with a hole in my life. As the following orchestra season approached, I looked forward with great anticipation, only to be disappointed not to be an active part of it. I attended concerts frequently, but I was depressed not to be playing. I eventually realized that it wasn't the music-making I missed as much as the daily contact with so many beautiful and talented musicians.

My job in the orchestra had been twofold. In addition to playing associate principal trumpet, for a number of years I also served as associate personnel manager. My personnel duties brought me into close personal contact with my colleagues. I was responsible for making sure all musicians were in place and on time, hiring replacements to cover for illness, calling "on stage" at rehearsals and concerts, and making announcements at rehearsals. I calculated musicians' payroll and attendance records. I was a conduit for communication between players, staff, and conductors. My backstage office always had tissues handy in case of emotional conversations or disputes. After retirement I missed my behind-the-scenes involvement in the running of the orchestra, whose members I considered an extension of my family.

My loneliness didn't last long. I had been invited to join a number of bands after I retired, but, reluctant to tie myself down to a weekly commitment, I had declined all the offers. One of my former students, Mike Schleicher, kept insisting, and I finally went with him to hear the Lake Wobegon® Brass Band. I was overwhelmed by the sound and the enthusiasm of this band, and I knew right then that if they would accept me, this was the band I wanted to join. A few weeks later another former student, Rick Perkins, invited me to lunch with the LWBB's conductor. After a warm and friendly luncheon I was offered a spot in the band, and I gladly accepted.

I was drawn to the LWBB for three reasons. First, the ensemble's musicianship is of exceptionally high quality. Many of the thirty-three members are band directors and music teachers in the Twin Cities, all of whom want to keep performing at an expert level. Second, the band rehearses only a few times before each set of performances. I could schedule around three annual concert runs. Third, and most important, the members of the LWBB were a loving, caring, thoughtful bunch of folks. They quickly became the new family of friends that I had been missing.

Celebrating daughter Judy's wedding

My new musical family became a critical source of inspiration and comfort during one of the darkest times of my life, when my youngest child, then in her 40s, developed a brain tumor and gradually succumbed. In the midst of my sorrow, I felt a virtual warm fuzzy blanket surrounding me with sincere love and concern. Gestures public and private touched me deeply, as when percussionist Donna Philippot dedicated a marathon race to Judy's memory.

Mike Halstenson, conductor of LWBB, is one of the best conductors among the hundreds I have observed over many years. Mike is always prepared, he runs efficient rehearsals and performances, and he has a comfortable rapport with his audiences. I'm not sure how or why it happened, but somewhere along the line Mike decided that I was fair game during concerts to tease about my age. When he introduced the audience to a modern version of "A Mighty Fortress Is Our God," he commented, "Back in the 1520s Martin Luther was planning to write only an *a cappella* version, but Ron told him, 'Martin, you need to add some trumpets and percussion.' And that's why we have the arrangement we will play today." He told a different audience that Martin Luther nailed the 95 Theses to the church door in Wittenberg with nails I had sold him at the local hardware store. Mike once introduced a Bach piece with, "We're going to play a piece written in 1695 by Bach, and Ron, who was helping him, said, 'Johann, you can't just write for harpsichord and organ. You need to jazz it up with trap set and brass.'" It was all in good fun, and I couldn't help but break out laughing every time. I asked other members of the band why Mike singled me out for this treatment, and they said it was because he loved me. I said at the time that a little less love might be preferred, but I think Mike knew how much I enjoyed the attention.

I felt the band's love again at a concert on my 86th birthday, when Mike publicly announced my retirement from the LWBB. In the middle of the concert I was overwhelmed by a glowing tribute from Mike and from Donna Philippot, complete with two cakes, one in honor of the retirement and one for my birthday. That was a wonderful way to end my playing career!

Apparently, I wasn't the only person who felt a personal closeness between me and the other LWBB members. The year after I retired from playing, the band invited me to accompany them on a mini-tour to northern Minnesota. When Chris Ravndal asked me to ride along I reminded him that I wasn't playing any more. Chris said that was OK, they just wanted my company. I couldn't think of a reason not to go (I was retired!), so I made the trip. It was like old times,

LWBB cornets with composer Philip Wilby at the International Trumpet Guild conference in Minneapolis, 2011

even up to the last evening. Mike and I were sitting in the hotel bar drinking a beer and musing about my being 87 years old. Mike remarked that in 13 years I would be 100, and suggested, "We ought to do it up even better than your last birthday. We will have a huge cake with a dancing girl pop out, balloons galore, fireworks, and just as they do in New York at New Year's, we'll have a big ball drop. When it hits the ground, we'll pull the plug." Even after I retired from the band, Mike got me one more time.

A group we call "Antique Brass," all retired brass players from the Minnesota Orchestra. Pictured here are (back row, L to R) me, Frank Winsor, Henry Charles Smith, Dave Kamminga, Bruce Rardin, (front row) Ron Ricketts, Mike Hipps, Clem Volpe, Ross Tolbert

An Irish Pub with Friends

After a Carnegie Hall concert in 1959, Bernie Adelstein (principal trumpet), Steve Zellmer (trombone), Frank Winsor (horn), and I went to Mulligan's pub a block from the hall for beer and snacks. The conversation centered around all the usual topics that young brass players discuss, such as conductors, musicians, mouthpieces, lead pipes, students, women, and young children.

Fast forward to 1997. We were back at Carnegie Hall to play a program featuring the Janacek Sinfonietta that includes fifteen trumpets. Bernie, who had by then retired from the Cleveland Orchestra, had been visiting his mother-in-law in Minneapolis, and agreed to play a week of concerts with the Minnesota Orchestra. We needed to take eleven extra trumpets on tour for the Janacek, so we invited Bernie to make the East Coast trip.

It wasn't planned, but after the Carnegie Hall concert the four of us (Bernie, Steve, Frank, and I) walked out of the hall together and ended up at the same pub, at the same table. Now the conversation changed to retirement

plans, reading glasses, grandkids, arthritis, medications, and friends and colleagues who had died. Nothing was mentioned of the topics discussed back in
1959. All of a sudden we hit a pause in the conversation, and we all sat back in
our chairs with the realization of what had just transpired. Thirty-eight years
had passed in the blink of an eye. We were older and on the other side of life,
still the best of friends (and still good-looking!), but substantially changed. We
drank our beers and laughed a lot, but we could feel a heaviness creep slowly
over the mood.

We lost Steve Zellmer two years after he left the orchestra, and Frank
Winsor more recently. I still play my trumpet but no longer professionally.
The Minnesota Orchestra is now populated with a new generation of talented
musicians. I earnestly hope that they all know how fortunate they are to be part
of such a marvelous institution.

Most of the fifteen trumpets needed to play the Janacek Sinfonietta: (Back row, L to R)
Clem Volpe, Chris Volpe, Dave Baldwin, Don Hakala, Bernie Adelstein, Ralph Schwartz,
Mike Hipps, Sylvan Pineault, me, (front row) Manny Laureano, Max Bonecutter, Dee Stewart,
Dave Chapman

Coda

Members of the Hasselmann clan at Minnehaha Park in 2018

With my sister Jean and mother Evelyn

With composer Leland Sateren on a cruise

With family members in Minneapolis

As a boy with my mother, sister, paternal grandparents, and maternal aunt and uncle

Visiting Laurie in Connecticut

CPSIA information can be obtained
at www.ICGtesting.com
Printed in the USA
LVHW011452231021
701271LV00007B/60/J